EARLY
CHRISTIAN EPITAPHS
FROM ATHENS

BY

JOHN S. CREAGHAN, S.J.

AND

A. E. RAUBITSCHEK

PUBLISHED BY

THEOLOGICAL STUDIES, WOODSTOCK, MARYLAND

1947

*This monograph is reprinted from Hesperia,
Volume XVI, with the aid of a grant from the
Maryland Province of the Society of Jesus.*

MANUFACTURED IN THE UNITED STATES OF AMERICA
BY J. H. FURST COMPANY, BALTIMORE, MARYLAND

SANCTAE
AGATHOCLIAE
SACRUM

FOREWORD

THE story of Christian Athens begins with the visit of St. Paul *ca.* 52 A.D., but the city never became one of the great centers of the new faith. Compared with the wealth of evidence, both literary and monumental, from pagan Athens, the Christian community has left but few traces of activity during the first five centuries of its existence. The records of scholars, bishops, apologists, and martyrs who studied, worked, or died in Athens are incomplete and have been transmitted, for the most part, through secondary sources. The general character of these accounts gives importance to the few, and otherwise insignificant, original monuments of that period: the early Christian epitaphs.

Even those periods of history for which literary evidence abounds have been considerably illuminated by the light of epigraphical evidence. For Christian Athens during the century which followed the official acceptance of Christianity one has to rely almost exclusively on the few humble tombstones which have survived. The study presented here attempts to show how much information may be drawn from this kind of material.

The study of ancient Greek writing, on clay, on stone, or on metal, has progressed with the study of Greek inscriptions, but its method has been necessarily different. While the epigraphist as historian is interested in the text, the epigraphist as archaeologist is concerned also with the actual script. For this purpose good and accurate illustrations of the original documents are needed. Only a few of the early Christian epitaphs from Athens have been adequately illustrated in previous publications, and the plates appended to this study fill therefore an urgent need. The script of the fifth century after Christ marks one of the last stages in the evolution of ancient Greek writing, and at the same time it marks an early step in the development which culminated in the creation of the medieval Slavic and Greek alphabets.

The publication of all Greek Christian inscriptions, or even of those from Athens alone, is a work still to be done; this monograph does not aim to be part of that larger enterprise, but it is valuable as an independent study and detailed examination of a group of closely related documents. It is fortunate that the authors have been able to combine their skills and special knowledge to make possible this joint publication.

BENJAMIN D. MERITT

Institute for Advanced Study

CONTENTS

(Plates I-X at End of Volume)

EARLY CHRISTIAN EPITAPHS FROM ATHENS

I. PREVIOUS PUBLICATIONS

THE FIRST extensive collection of the early Christian inscriptions from Attica was made by S. A. Koumanoudes.[1] The significance of his publication lies in the fact that he separated the early Christian inscriptions of the fourth, fifth, and sixth centuries from the Byzantine inscriptions of the following centuries.[2] He excluded these later inscriptions because of the many ligatures and other peculiarities and difficulties in script which seemed to require a separate treatment (*op. cit.*, Foreword, p. 2). This distinction made by Koumanoudes was accepted by C. Bayet whose dissertation *De Titulis Atticae Christianis Antiquissimis, Commentatio Historica et Epigraphica* (abbreviated: Bayet), 1878, is still the best treatment of this subject, although it has found little attention.

Bayet began his investigation by writing a commentary on many of the published documents, to which he added a few recently found inscriptions.[3] These articles, rather than his more comprehensive dissertation, were used by W. Dittenberger for the edition of the early Christian inscriptions in *I.G.*, III, 3435-3547, published in 1882.[4] Dittenberger added seventeen more inscriptions to the number already known, but he failed to include several others which were published only by Bayet (nos. 10, 11, 13, 56, 60, 79, 81, 82, 84, 87, 95, 106).[5] There are, moreover, several minor differences in the texts of the four inscriptions published separately and independently by Bayet and Dittenberger.[6] Dittenberger also omitted an inscription from Laureion published by S. A. Koumanoudes, Ἀθήναιον, IX, 1880, pp. 171-172, no. 2.

[1] Ἀττικῆς Ἐπιγραφαὶ Ἐπιτύμβιοι, 1871, nos. 3540-3623. Sixteen of these eighty-five inscriptions had been previously published in the *Corpus Inscriptionum Graecarum* (I, 965; IV, 9303, 9307-9316, 9318-9320). Although Kirchhoff considered *C.I.G.*, IV, 9317 a Christian epitaph (because it was found with other similar stones near the Church of Λαμπριώτισσα), Koumanoudes placed it (no. 2270) among the pagan monuments. C. Bayet (*op. cit. supra*) tentatively included this epitaph in his collection (no. 120), but he questioned the reason given by Kirchhoff. Dittenberger (*I.G.*, III, 1455) and Kirchner (*I.G.*, II², 11153) placed it among the pagan inscriptions; compare L. Robert, *Rev. de Phil.*, XIV, 1943, p. 188.

[2] He does, however, include two inscriptions of a later period. No. 3572 is dated in the year 936, but the text is uncertain; no. 3587 is dated in the year 1064. For a recent discussion of these late inscriptions, see V. Laurent, *Études Byzantines*, I, pp. 63 ff. [we did not consult this book].

[3] *B.C.H.*, I, 1877, pp. 391-408; II, 1878, pp. 31-35 and 162-166.

[4] Dittenberger also published several Christian epigrams in *I.G.*, III, 1383-1387, and three other Christian epitaphs in *I.G.*, III, 1427, 1428, and 3516 *a* (in the addenda on p. 306). Eight (*I.G.*, III, 3437 + 3481 *b*, 3438, 3465, 3487, 3502, 3513, 3516 *a*, and 3517) are republished below, Nos. I to VIII.

[5] Six of these (nos. 11, 13, 79, 81, 87 and 95) are republished below, Nos. X to XV.

[6] 1. The inscription published by Bayet, no. 22, and by Dittenberger, *I.G.*, III, 3488, is now

In the same year in which Dittenberger's *Inscriptiones Graecae*, III, appeared, P. Konstantinides published sixteen Christian inscriptions in Παρνασσός, VI, 1882, pp. 80-85. Most of these inscriptions were found in the year 1877, in the Asklepieion and in various other places in Athens.[7] In the same volume of Παρνασσός (p. 252), J. Ch. Dragarses published a Christian inscription from the Piraeus.

One of the most important Christian epitaphs was found in 1888 during excavations conducted on the slope of Mount Lykabettos, at 26 Tsakalof Street.[8] It is the tombstone of Bishop Klematios, dated in the fifth century by the letter forms of the inscription and by the architectural fragments which were found at the same time.[9]

In Δελτίον τῆς Χριστιανικῆς Ἀρχαιολογικῆς Ἑταιρείας, I, 1892, pp. 67-68 (the third inscription is pagan; see below, note 22) and II, 1894, p. 89 (a text from Mt. Lykabettos), several other epitaphs were published by G. Lampakes. A few years later, K. M. Konstantopoulos' Ἀνέκδοτοι ἐπιγραφαὶ ἐπιτύμβιοι χριστιανικῶν χρόνων appeared in Ἁρμονία, 1900, pp. 19-37, nos. 1-38 (abbreviated: *Harmonia*).

Four of the inscriptions published by Konstantopoulos (nos. 2, 19, 20, 31) had already been included in Bayet (nos. 79, 81, 95, 87).[10] Four (nos. 13, 16, 17, 26), actually found in Corinth, were originally published by A. N. Skias, Ἐφ. Ἀρχ., 1893, cols. 125-127 (nos. 22, 18, 20, 17), and republished in *I.G.*, IV, 409, 411, 413, 404, and in the *Corpus der Griechisch-Christlichen Inschriften von Hellas* (abbreviated *C.G.-C.I.*), I, 1 (Isthmos-Korinthos, edited by N. A. Bees), nos. 44, 41, 56, 42.[11]

in the Epigraphical Museum at Athens (E.M. 9943). Dittenberger failed to indicate the traces of a cross (flanked by two other crosses? See below, note 74) above the inscription. Bayet's restoration of the name (Φιλ[έα]) is preferable to Dittenberger's (Φίλω[νος]), for the lower part of the epsilon is actually preserved. On the other hand, Dittenberger's reading [Κ]οιμητήριον is correct.

2. For a discussion of *I.G.*, III, 3517 = Bayet, no. 23, see below, No. VIII.

3. The inscription published by Bayet, no. 61, and by Dittenberger, *I.G.*, III, 3474, is now in the Epigraphical Museum (E.M. 9903). The text of this columnar grave monument as given by Dittenberger is correct, for the first letter of the third line is clearly a gamma.

4. For a discussion of *I.G.*, III, 3487 = Bayet, no. 83, see below, No. IV.

[7] The epitaph published by Konstantinides, *loc. cit.*, p. 81, no. 1, was already included by Bayet (no. 10); N. A. Bees, *C.G.-C.I.* (see p. 24), I, 1, p. 91, apparently thought that they were two different inscriptions. Since Bayet did not illustrate this stone with a drawing (and probably never saw it?), the text of Konstantinides may be accepted. The inscription published as no. 8 is now in the Epigraphical Museum (E.M. 5680); no. 11 is republished below, No. XVI.

[8] See Neroutsos, Δελτίον τῆς Ἱστορικῆς Ἑταιρείας, III, 1889, p. 71; J. Strzygowski, *Röm. Quartalschrift*, 1890, p. 1; G. A. Soteriou, Εὑρετήριον, I, p. 56, fig. 43; *Guide²*, p. 43; *Byz.-Neugr. Jahrb.*, X, 1933-1934, p. 179, fig. 8.

[9] For the possible identification of the Bishop with Klematios mentioned in *I.G.*, II², 13224, see below, p. 10.

[10] These are republished below, Nos. XII-XV.

[11] These stones were first brought to the Museum of the Archaeological Society (where Konstantopoulos copied them, perhaps unaware of their provenience; see also note 162), and were later transferred to the Epigraphical Museum (E.M. 9963, 9959, 9960, 9957). In *Harmonia*, no. 13 (Skias, no. 22 = *I.G.*, IV, 409 = *C.G.-C.I.*, I, 1, 44), the first preserved line should be read and

Several others (nos. 14, 18 + 33, 35-38) are of a later period.[12] In spite of this, his publication, which is hardly accessible outside Greece,[13] ranks with Bayet's as one of the outstanding contributions in the field. The many tombstones which he publishes for the first time are illustrated by drawings and are described in detail. We republish seven of them (nos. 3, 4, 5, 6, 9, 10, and 15 = Nos. XVII to XXIII) and illustrate two others (nos. 12 and 22 on Plates VIII and X) with photographs taken from squeezes, not so much to correct his texts as to make our study of the early Christian inscriptions from Athens more nearly complete.

No new collection of the Christian inscriptions from Attica has since appeared, but a number of recently found documents have been published in various periodicals. Two stones found during the excavations of the Odeion of Perikles, and thus coming from the Christian cemetery in the old sanctuary of Asklepios, were published by P. Kastriotes, ’Αρχ. ’Εφ., 1914, p. 166, nos. 4 and 5.[14] During the excavations conducted on the northeast slope of the Areopagus, G. A. Soteriou found, and subsequently published in ’Αρχ. Δελτ., II, 1916, p. 142, fig. 16, one early Christian epitaph which may belong to the same cemetery as the Christian tombstones found in the near-by Agora.[15] A Christian inscription from Laureion was published by G. K. Zesios, ’Επιγραφαὶ Χριστιανῶν χρόνων τῆς ‘Ελλάδος, 1917, p. 17 (reprinted in the author's collected essays, Σύμμικτα, p. 13, note 1). An interesting Christian tombstone was found in February, 1916, near the Theatre of Dionysos (thus also belonging to the Asklepieion cemetery), and was published by A. C. Chatses, ’Αρχ. ’Εφ., 1925-1926, p. 97, fig. 2. The inscription was engraved on the back of a fragment of an Attic prytany list (I.G., II², 1806a) dated ca. 190-200 after Christ.[16]

Most of the Christian inscriptions which were found during the 19th century and which were originally kept in various places were transferred toward the end of the century to the then newly established Epigraphical Museum in Athens, and are still there, together with the pagan inscriptions. Judging from the collection of squeezes kept at the Institute for Advanced Study at Princeton, some of these inscrip-

restored as ’Αγαθοκλ[(ῆς or εία) μη]νί. For the abbreviations of the last line, see also Corinth, VIII, 1, no. 147, and for the guide lines on this stone, see below, note 139.

[12] Konstantopoulos himself observed that nos. 35-38 are later than the seventh century. The abbreviations used in no. 14 (E.M. 9995) make it likely that this document is also of a date later than the sixth century. The same applies to no. 18 (E.M. 9974) which belongs to the same stone as no. 33 (E.M. 9985), together with an unpublished fragment, the inventory number of which (E.M. 9975) indicates that this fragment has already been combined with no. 18.

[13] For rare Greek books kept in American libraries, see P .W. Topping, Byzantion, XV, 1940-1941, pp. 434-436.

[14] The illustration, fig. 23, shows that the reading of no. 5, as printed by Kastriotes, should be slightly corrected: [κυμητή]|ριον| Στεφά|νο(υ) κ(αὶ) Σο|λομω|νίδος. For the use of the ligature omikron upsilon and of the abbreviated form of καί, see below, notes 66 and 63.

[15] See below, notes 80 and 130.

[16] For the text of the Christian inscription, see below, note 41.

tions do not seem to have been published. After the opening of the Byzantine Museum, in 1914, the more recently discovered Christian inscriptions, and apparently also some of the older pieces, were placed there. The *Guide* of this Museum, published by G. Soteriou, contains discussions and illustrations of some of the 33 assembled documents.[17]

Finally, there may be mentioned the Christian inscriptions found by O. Broneer on the North Slope of the Akropolis and published in *Hesperia*, as well as a new inscription from the Pnyx which is probably Christian.[18]

Of the Christian inscriptions found during the excavations of the Agora, only one has been published thus far (*Hesperia*, XIII, 1944, p. 265, no. 19). Most of the other documents are published below, Nos. 1-34.

II. ARRANGEMENT OF THE MATERIAL

Bayet observed (pp. 29-31) that the Christian gravestones of Athens may be separated into groups according to the place of discovery. He rightly assumed, moreover, that the various regions in which Christian tombstones were found must have contained Christian cemeteries. The early date of two of these cemeteries has been confirmed by recent investigations.[19] The name of the saint, to whose church the cemetery on Mount Lykabettos belonged, is unknown, but the burial ground located in the Asklepios sanctuary may have been attached to a church dedicated to Saint Andrew; see No. XI. The great number of early Christian epitaphs found in the Agora excavations, at a considerable distance from any of the three areas mentioned above, points to the existence of an early Christian cemetery in or near the Agora itself. Two early Christian churches are known in this region,[20] yet no early Christian burials have been found near these two churches.[21] On the other hand, the church of St. Agathokleia is known from two early epitaphs, one of which was found in the

---

[17] See *Guide*¹ (1924), p. 21 and plate 4 (after p. 40); *Guide*² (1931), pp. 42-43; compare also G. A. Soteriou, Εὑρετήριον τῶν Μεσαιωνικῶν Μνημείων τῆς Ἑλλάδος (abbreviated: Εὑρετήριον), I, pp. 25-26, fig. 2 (on p. 10), and pp. 55-56, fig. 43.

[18] See II, 1933, p. 414, no. 39, fig. 89; IV, 1935, p. 186, no. 53, fig. 76 = XI, 1942, p. 303, no. 62 (see below, note 33); VII, 1938, pp. 262-263, fig. 88 etc.; *Suppl.* VII, pp. 10-11, no. 16 (cf. L. Robert, *R.E.G.*, LVII, 1944, p. 208, no. 90): Ὀνησᾶ μνήμη καὶ Ἐπαγάθης. For μνήμη = μνῆμα, see W. K. Prentice, *Greek and Latin Inscriptions* (1908), no. 278. See also note 31, below.

[19] For the Asklepieion area, see G. A. Soteriou, Εὑρετήριον, I, pp. 47-48; for the Lykabettos area, see *ibid.*, pp. 55-56. The many Christian epitaphs found in the old pagan Dipylon cemetery show that this ancient Athenian burial ground was also used by the Christians. The excavations of the only Byzantine Church in this region, Hagia Trias, have, unfortunately, revealed no early Christian remains; see K. Kübler, *Arch. Anz.*, 1932, cols. 184 and 187.

[20] The temple of Hephaistos converted into a church of St. George (W. B. Dinsmoor, *Hesperia*, Supplement V, p. 11, with bibliography), and the so-called Μεγάλη Παναγία built into the library of Hadrian (A. Xyngopoulos, Εὑρετήριον, II, 88-89).

[21] See A. Mommsen's remarks (*Ath. Christ.*, pp. 99-100, note 2) on Pittakes' readings of Ἐφ. Ἀρχ., 1853, nos. 1599 and 1600.

Agora (below, No. 5). It may be suggested that the Christian tombstones found in this region once stood in the cemetery of St. Agathokleia.

The classification of the Christian tombstones according to the cemeteries to which they may have belonged is one of the features of Bayet's dissertation. Koumanoudes arranged the inscriptions which he published according to the alphabetical order of the names which occur on them, pointing out (Foreword, p. 7) that they contained for the most part neither ethnics nor demotics διὰ τὸ ἔχειν τοὺς χριστιανοὺς πατρίδα τὴν ἄνω Ἰερουσαλήμ.[22] The new *Corpus der Griechisch-Christlichen Inschriften* (see below, p. 24) has the same arrangement, but begins with the longer texts which contain imprecations and records of sale. Dittenberger, on the other hand, grouped together the inscriptions with the same formula (κοιμητήριον, οἰκητήριον, etc.). As the obvious result of this arrangement the predominance of the word κοιμητήριον is evident.

III. KOIMHTHPION

Bayet has already called attention to the frequent occurrence of κοιμητήριον on Christian epitaphs (pp. 43-46), pointing out that the use of this word, meaning a single tomb, is restricted almost entirely to Thessaly, Attica, and Corinthia. Recent findings in these three regions tend to confirm his observations.[23] It should be noted, however, that κοιμητήριον occurs frequently on the Christian tombstones of Phrygia.[24] A single Christian epitaph from Spain begins with the word κυμετέριον.[25]

F. J. M. De Waele and N. A. Bees have devoted several pages to a thorough discussion of the history and usage of this term.[26] Bees claims that κοιμητήριον occurs also on pagan inscriptions in the meaning of burial place (*op. cit.*, p. 70), but the two examples which he cites are by no means certainly pagan.[27] The purely Christian

[22] The only supposedly Christian inscription containing a demotic was published by G. Lampakes, Δελτίον τῆς Χριστιανικῆς Ἀρχαιολογικῆς Ἑταιρείας, I, 1892, p. 68. This inscription, however, is not a Christian epitaph, and it is now republished among the pagan documents (*I.G.*, II², 6785); for the place of discovery of this stone, see A. Xyngopoulos, Εὑρετήριον, II, p. 108. For the occurrence and the meaning of πρεσβύτερος, see A. E. Raubitschek, *Hesperia*, Supplement VII, p. 4.

[23] See for example N. I. Giannopoulos, Ἐπετηρὶς Ἑταιρείας Βυζαντινῶν Σπουδῶν (abbreviated: Ἐπετηρίς), XII, 1936, pp. 401 and 403; *Corinth*, VIII, 1, pp. 93-101, nos. 137-154; *C.G.–C.I.*, I, 1, nos. 17, 31-34, 37, 39, 43, 45-47, 49, 51, 54, 62-65.

[24] See, for example, W. M. Ramsay, *J.H.S.*, IV, 1883, pp. 407 (no. 23), 429 (no. 39), 430 (no. 40); *Cities and Bishoprics of Phrygia*, II, pp. 530 (no. 376), 539 (no. 400), 558-559 (no. 445), 719 (no. 654), 720 (no. 655), 733 (no. 659); M. Ramsay, *Aberdeen Univ. Studies*, XX, 1906, p. 89, no. 58; W. M. Calder, *J.R.S.*, XIV, 1924, p. 87 (no. 5); W. H. Buckler, W. M. Calder, C. W. M. Cox, *J.R.S.*, XVI, 1926, pp. 55 (no. 172), 57 (no. 175); W. H. Buckler and W. M. Calder, *Monumenta Asiae Minoris Antiquae* (abbreviated: *M.A.M.A.*), VI, p. 86 (no. 232).

[25] C. Wessel, *Inscr. Gr. Christ. Vet. Occid.*, p. 18, no. 104; for coemeterium *T.L.L. s.v.*

[26] *C.G.–C.I.*, I, 1, pp. 38-39 and 68-72; compare also O. Merlier, *B.C.H.*, LIV, 1930, pp. 233-234, and A. C. Rush, *Death and Burial in Christian Antiquity*, pp. 12, 16 and 20.

[27] *A.J.A.*, VII, 1903, p. 58, no. 36 = *Corinth*, VIII, 1, no. 155; *Papers of the Am. School at*

character of this word, when used to signify a burial place, has been discussed else-where.[28] " To the Christian," to use P. Gardner's words (*New Chapters*, p. 332), " the place of interment is no longer a tomb, but a sleeping place." The use of κοιμητήριον and coemeterium has a deep spiritual significance which is beautifully explained by Saint John Chrysostom in his sermon εἰς τὸ ὄνομα τοῦ κοιμητηρίου (J. P. Migne, *Patrologia Graeca*, XLIX, cols. 393-394). The pertinent passages may be quoted in full: Διὰ τοῦτο καὶ αὐτὸς ὁ τόπος κοιμητήριον ὠνόμασται, ἵνα μάθῃς ὅτι οἱ τετελευτηκότες καὶ ἐνταῦθα κείμενοι οὐ τεθνήκασι, ἀλλὰ κοιμῶνται καὶ καθεύδουσι. Πρὸ μὲν γὰρ τῆς παρουσίας Χριστοῦ ὁ θάνατος θάνατος ἐκαλεῖτο· . . . ἐπειδὴ δὲ ἦλθεν ὁ Χριστός, καὶ ὑπὲρ ζωῆς τοῦ κόσμου ἀπέθανεν, οὐκέτι θάνατος καλεῖται λοιπὸν ὁ θάνατος, ἀλλὰ ὕπνος καὶ κοίμησις. . . . Ὅρα πανταχοῦ ὕπνον καλούμενον τὸν θάνατον· διὰ τοῦτο καὶ ὁ τόπος κοιμητήριον ὠνόμασται· χρήσιμον γὰρ ἡμῖν καὶ τὸ ὄνομα, καὶ φιλοσοφίας γέμον πολλῆς. Ὅταν τοίνυν ἄγῃς ἐνταῦθα νεκρόν, μὴ κατάκοπτε σεαυτόν· οὐ γὰρ πρὸς θάνατον, ἀλλὰ πρὸς ὕπνον αὐτὸν ἄγεις. Ἀρκεῖ σοι τοῦτο τὸ ὄνομα εἰς παραμυθίαν συμ-φορᾶς. Μάθε ποῦ ἄγεις· εἰς κοιμητήριον· καὶ πότε ἄγεις· μετὰ τὸν τοῦ Χριστοῦ θάνατον, ὅτε τὰ νεῦρα ἐξεκόπη τοῦ θανάτου.

This sentiment, which might well have been expressed before Chrysostom, may have given rise to the use of the word κοιμητήριον on Christian tombstones. The epigraphical evidence tends to show that the use of κοιμητήριον for a single tomb prevailed in Greek lands about the time of Chrysostom, while it occurred in Egypt and in Phrygia as early as 250 A.D. (See W. M. Ramsay, *Cities and Bishoprics of Phrygia*, II, p. 559). In contrast to the other words used for tomb (τόπος, θήκη, μνημόριον, μνῆμα, and others), κοιμητήριον (and οἰκητήριον, κατοικητήριον) signifies a Christian burial.[29] If it is used also on Jewish stones, this only indicates a Christian influence.[30]

IV. FORMULAE

The majority of the Christian epitaphs from Attica, as already emphasized, begin with the word κοιμητήριον followed by the name of the deceased in the genitive. Some of these monuments record the death of only one person, while others are dedicated to the memory of husband and wife, whose names are connected by καί.[31] This close

Athens, III, 1884-1885, pp. 145-146, no. 250. For the pagan equation of death and sleep, see R. Lattimore, *Themes in Greek and Latin Epitaphs*, p. 164.

[28] See W. M. Ramsay, *Cities and Bishoprics of Phrygia*, II, pp. 488, 495, 515, 518 and 559, and A. C. Rush, *op. cit.*, pp. 20-21.

[29] Compare Bees, *op. cit.*, pp. 84-85; Rush, *op. cit.*, pp. 20-21.

[30] See P. J.-B. Frey, *Corpus Inscr. Iud.* (abbreviated: *C.I.I.*), I, pp. 515-516, nos. 712 and 713 (*I.G.*, III, 3545 and 3546); compare Bees, *op. cit.*, pp. 70-71.

[31] Several of these epitaphs omit the conjunction καί; see *I.G.*, III, 3518, Nos. II, XV. *I.G.*, II², 7119 and 10934 may be Christian since no similar pagan inscriptions from Athens connect the names with καί; for the abbreviation of καί in *I.G.*, II², 10934, see below, pp. 11-12.

association of married couples, even in death, seems to be distinctly Christian. Ordinarily, the husband's name is mentioned first, but the reverse order is also found, possibly indicating that the wife died first.[32] Two epitaphs, which contain the names of two men, indicate that father and son were also buried side by side.[33] There is one doubtful instance in which the death of two women is recorded on one and the same stone, with no indication of their mutual relationship (*I.G.*, III, 3480).

There is one example of a double tombstone on which two inscriptions are engraved by different hands (No. V). Similarly, a Megarian stone published by Bayet (no. 109 = *I.G.*, VII, 170-171) consists of two epitaphs.[34] In Attica there may be another example of such a double tombstone if Koumanoudes' text of *C.I.G.*, 965 (*op. cit.*, no. 3593 = Bayet, no. 104 = *I.G.*, III, 3457 = *I.G.*, II², 13240) can be trusted.[35] It may be noted, incidentally, that the use of double tombstones by the early Christians is not confined to Greece.[36]

The shortest Christian tomb inscriptions give merely the name of the deceased in the genitive. These should be distinguished from the otherwise similar pagan documents with the name in the nominative.[37] It is reasonable to assume that these genitives depend on the word κοιμητήριον which is implied. In another group, the old pagan formula ἐνθάδε κεῖται is used; a typically Christian variant of this phrase is ἐνθάδε κατοικεῖ (see No. XIII).

Many of the pagan epitaphs, even of the latest period, contain the names of the father and the demotic or ethnic of the deceased, but the Christian inscriptions rarely mention father's name or ethnic.[38] No known Christian inscription contains a demotic; see note 22.

Numerous Christian epitaphs proudly record the occupation of the deceased, and thus are distinguished from the pagan stones which rarely mention occupations. From these tombstones we learn that the Christians of Athens were engaged in substantial

[32] *I.G.*, III, 3467, 3515 (see below, note 131); 3546 (Jewish); Nos. V and 17 below; compare note 33. For the common burial of husband and wife in pagan times, see Lattimore, *op. cit.*, pp. 247-250.

[33] *I.G.*, III, 3449 and No. 1. In another document (*Hesperia*, IV, 1935, p. 186, no. 53, fig. 76 = *Hesperia*, XI, 1942, p. 303, no. 62), the names of two men (brothers, possibly twins, as Meritt suggests) have been restored, but the first name may equally well have been that of a woman: Μελιτί[ας]; see the commentary on No. XXI. Normally the husband's name is mentioned first; compare however note 32. A tombstone from Megara (*I.G.*, VII, 174; see below, note 68) also contains the names of two men.

[34] Bees, *op. cit.*, p. 91, aptly remarks: in *I.G.*, III nicht vorhanden.

[35] See also the commentary on No. 3.

[36] See Bayet, p. 32; compare Jalabert and Mouterde, *Inscriptions Grecques et Latines de la Syrie*, I, nos. 182, 188; II, no. 333; D. M. Robinson, *T.A.P.A.*, LVII, 1926, p. 198, nos. 2 and 3, and plate II, fig. 2.

[37] A single Christian epitaph (*Harmonia*, no. 30), which is now kept in the Epigraphical Museum (E.M. 9984), has the name in the nominative.

[38] See, however, *I.G.*, III, 3483, 3529, 3547; *I.G.*, II², 13216 and No. 26.

and necessary work. Bayet has already called attention to this fact, and he has listed
the various professions that were known from the stones which he published (p. 38,
note 5).[39] In addition to the occupations listed by Bayet, we know now that among
the Christians of Athens there were also cutlers (No. XV), physicians (*I.G.*, III,
3482), coppersmiths,[40] and gravediggers.[41] The occupation of two other Christians
is given as σιρικάριος.[42] We are unable to decide whether this term means here " silk-
worker " or " silk-merchant "; in Constantinople, the guild of the σηρικάριοι included
both clothiers and dyers.[43] It is interesting to see that Athens apparently participated
in the imperial trade or manufacture of silk. Another epitaph records the death of
Ioullianos of whom it is said: τέχνης κεντητῆς ⌈κ⌉αλῶς φρε[ν]ήσας, "a man well
skilled in the art of mosaics." [44] Another Christian was a maker of πίνακες, if our
interpretation of the word πενακᾶς in *I.G.*, III, 3459 is correct; see below, note 107.

The most interesting of these documents mentioning occupations are the epitaphs
of the members of the various grades of the clergy: they are, of course, without
parallel among the pagan inscriptions. Bayet (p. 38, note 5) has already called
attention to the offices of presbyter (see also No. 4), deacon, and reader (see also
No. 5) which are recorded on Attic tombstones. In an inscription published below
(No. 2) the office of subdeacon is mentioned for the first time in Athens.[45] Another
epitaph (No. 5) records the death of Andreas, reader of the Church of St. Agathokleia.
Readers are known from other epitaphs, none of which, however, mention the church
with which they were associated.[46] It may now be presumed that each of the early
Christian churches of Athens had its own reader. Other officials (subdeacons, deacons

---

[39] The evidence gathered by A. T. Geogehan (*The Attitude towards Labor*, pp. 225-228) from
the Latin inscriptions (mainly from Rome) could have been greatly augmented, had the author
included in his study the inscriptions from Greece, and especially those from Athens.

[40] G. Lampakes, Δελτίον τῆς Χριστιανικῆς Ἑταιρείας, II, 1894, p. 89; for the spelling χαρκέ[ω]ς.
see below, note 125; compare J. Keil and A. Wilhelm, *M.A.M.A.*, III, p. 150, no. 329.

[41] A. C. Chatses, Ἀρχ. Ἐφ., 1925-1926, p. 97, fig. 2. The reading and restoration of this inscription are puzzling because of the occurrence of two peculiar letter forms, and because the cross
above the preserved part of the text probably marked the center of the first line. We suggest
restoring θήκη Μενοι[--- δε]κανοῦ. For the δεκανοί, gravediggers, see E. Hanton, *Byzantion*, IV,
1927-1928, pp. 72-74; *Sardis*, VII, 1, no. 173; N. A. Bees, *C.G.–C.I.*, I, 1, pp. 81-82.

[42] See the epitaph illustrated by G. A. Soteriou, Εὑρετήριον, I, p. 10, fig. 2 (spelled σιρηκάριος;
see note 118) and No. VI; compare Bees, *op. cit.*, p. 62. A tombstone from Rome mentions a
σιρικοποιός; see C. Wessel, *Inscr. Gr. Christianae Veteres Occidentis*, p. 27, no. 154.

[43] See R. S. Lopez, *Speculum*, XX, 1945, p. 8 and note 2.

[44] O. Broneer, *Hesperia*, VII, 1938, pp. 262-263, fig. 88; compare N. Bees, *Byz. Jb.*, XIV,
1938, p. 292.

[45] See E. Hanton, *Byzantion*, IV, 1927-1928, p. 74; *Inscriptiones Creticae*, I, p. 32, no. 6
(Ἀρχ. Δελτ., II, 1916, p. 11); compare *Cambridge Medieval History*, I, p. 150.

[46] See E. Hanton, *Byzantion*, IV, 1927-1928, pp. 63-64; compare, however, the numerous
examples quoted by F. Preisigke, *Wörterbuch*, III, p. 397, *s. v.* ἀναγνώστης.

and presbyters) may also have been attached to separate churches, all of whom were under the bishop (ἐπίσκοπος).[47]

The only Attic epitaph of an early Christian bishop (see above, p. 2) refers to the office of ἐπίσκοπος with a participle: ὁ ἐν ὁσίοις ἐπισκοπήσας Κλημάτιος. Attention should be called here to another Athenian epitaph which contains the participle περιο-δεύσας. It was first published by Dittenberger in *I.G.*, III, 1375, later by N. A. Bees (*Rh. Mus.*, LXIX, 1914, pp. 744-746), without reference to the previous publication, and finally by Kirchner (*I.G.*, II², 13167), who in turn referred only to Dittenberger. The stone is now in the Epigraphical Museum (E.M. 9866). Bees, who alone gave the correct reading, interpreted περιοδεύσας as referring to the occupation of a physician, and this meaning of the verb is well attested. It is possible, however, that this participle may refer to the clerical office of περιοδευτής, which is mentioned in three inscriptions from Syria; see W. K. Prentice, *Greek and Latin Inscriptions* (1908), nos. 7, 288 and 336 a (?). Prentice remarked (*op. cit.*, p. 35) that the περιοδευτής was an ecclesiastical inspector with a rank intermediate between that of bishop and that of presbyter, who directed the erection of church buildings. It is possible, therefore, that the Attic inscription is Christian. In addition to the similarity in the participial construction of this inscription and of the bishop's epitaph the περιοδεύσας text resembles the early Christian inscriptions in several other respects. There is an abbreviation mark over the final omega of βροτῶ(ν) in line 1, and a leaf at the end of the last line (Bees failed to record these); see below, notes 69 and 98. The nu in lines 3, 4 and 5, and the rho in line 5 are similar to the corresponding letters of No. XII.

A feature common to the late pagan and early Christian epitaphs is the addition of threats or imprecations directed against those who might open and violate the grave.[48] This similarity in the formulae has led to considerable confusion in the publication and classification of the documents of this type.

The twenty pagan documents from Athens which contain threats or imprecations are published in *I.G.*, II², 13209-13228 (*Tituli sepulcrales cum diris et poenarum sanctionibus, B. Monumenta reliqua*). Three of these (*I.G.*, II², 13225, 13226, 13228) do not really belong to this group; three others (*I.G.*, II², 13212, 13218, 13221) are not Attic, but were brought to the Piraeus from Perinthus, and the Attic origin of

---

[47] See *Cambridge Medieval History*, I, p. 149. For examples of deacons who were attached to particular churches, see F. Preisigke, *Wörterbuch*, III, pp. 399 and 405, *s. vv.* διάκονος and πρεσβύτερος.

[48] For a discussion of curses found on Christian tombstones, see J. Merkel, *Über die sogenannten Sepulcralmulten*, pp. 40-42, 46-47; G. Millet, *B.C.H.*, XXIX, 1905, pp. 65-66; N. I. Giannopoulos, Ἐπετηρίς, XII, 1936, p. 405; N. A. Bees, *op. cit.*, pp. 32-33; compare also W. Larfeld, *Griechische Epigraphik*³, p. 452, no. 265; Lattimore, *op. cit.*, pp. 108-118; D. M. Robinson, *Cl. J.*, XL, 1945, pp. 38-41. Special attention should be given in this connection to the edict of Augustus which protected tombs (*S.E.G.*, VIII, no. 13, with bibliography).

one (*I.G.*, II², 13217) does not seem to be well attested.[49] Four of the remaining thirteen inscriptions (*I.G.*, II², 13216, 13223, 13219, 13224) are, according to L. Robert,[50] either Christian, or belong to the end of the third or the fourth century after Christ. The Christian character of *I.G.*, II², 13223 (E.M. 12592, according to our squeeze) was deduced from Kirchner's restoration μὴ τῶι θεῶ[ι λόγον δῶις], but this restoration is by no means certain. The letter forms of the inscription do not easily allow a date after the middle of the third century, and it does not seem certain, moreover, that this epigram belongs to a tomb monument. *I.G.*, II², 13216 B and C has already been recognized as a Christian epitaph not only by Kirchner but also by Koumanoudes and by Bayet, who republished the text (no. 42) ; see, however, note 105. The date of *I.G.*, II², 13224 cannot be determined with accuracy unless it is possible to identify the master of Primos, Klematios, with the bishop Klematios whose tombstone was found in Athens.[51] *I.G.*, II², 13222 is a Christian epitaph (overlooked by Robert), as we have shown (No. IX). Robert suggested as date of *I.G.*, II², 13219 the end of the third century. We have been able to join this fragment with another which was originally thought to be Christian (No. XX). Robert, finally, called attention [52] to a Latin epitaph (*I.G.*, II², 13213) of a Roman soldier, which contains a Greek subscript forbidding destruction of the tomb.[53] There are, therefore, only ten examples of pagan documents which certainly belong to this group,[54] to which may be added No. XIX of this publication.

It is interesting to note that all but two of the fourteen Attic Christian inscriptions which contain curses are introduced by conditional clauses, such as εἰ δέ τις τολμήσει (or ἐπιτηδεύσει), or by corresponding relative pronouns.[55] The two remaining texts have participles instead of relative or conditional clauses.

A characteristic distinction between the pagan and Christian examples from Athens lies in the fact that most of the former impose fines upon the violator, while the latter generally exact other penalties.[56] Three epitaphs threaten the transgressor

[49] See L. Robert, *Rev. de Phil.*, XVIII, 1944, pp. 38-40, 48; J. and L. Robert, *R.E.G.*, LVI, 1943, pp. 336-337, no. 18.

[50] *Loc. cit.*, pp. 37-38.

[51] See notes 8 and 9; compare note 125.

[52] *Loc. cit.*, p. 38, note 2.

[53] An examination of the squeeze reveals that the first preserved letter of the penultimate line is a lambda and not a mu. The restoration [τὸν βω]μὸν τοῦτον should therefore be changed to [τὸν τίτ]λον τοῦτον, which also better fills the available space; compare D. M. Robinson, *T.A.P.A.*, LVII, 1926, pp. 199 (no. 4) and 200 (No. 5) ; *C.G.–C.I.*, I, 1, no. 30, line 10. The Latin name in line 5 may be restored as [L. Alf]eius Maximus, with reference to another unpublished epitaph from Eleusis which was set up by the same man.

[54] *I.G.*, II², 13209-11, 13213-15, 13219 + *Harmonia*, no. 6 (= No. XX), 13220, 13224, 13227.

[55] Bayet, nos. 42, 60, 84; *I.G.*, III, 3509, 3543; Koumanoudes, ᾽Αθήναιον, IX, 1880, p. 171, no. 2; G. Lampakes, Δελτίον τῆς Χριστιανικῆς ᾽Αρχαιολογικῆς ῾Εταιρείας, I, 1892, p. 67; G. K. Zesios, Σύμμικτα, p. 13, note 1; Nos. IX, XII, XVI, and 15.

[56] See, however, Nos. XX and 15.

with the curse of Judas (*I.G.*, III, 1428; *Harmonia*, no. 1; G. K. Zesios, Σύμμικτα, p. 13, note 1). Two others warn the violator that he must make a reckoning before God (Koumanoudes, Ἀθήναιον, IX, 1880, p. 171, no. 2; *I.G.*, III, 3509) and one (Bayet, no. 42 = *I.G.*, II², 13216) mentions the wrath of God.

These various types of early Christian epitaphs in general continued the pagan tradition, and lasted from the fifth to the seventh centuries. At about the end of this period, two new formulae which had been employed only rarely in earlier times began to be used more and more frequently, and the older formulae disappeared completely.[57] A study of the terminology, therefore, tends to show that a break in the tradition occurred in the seventh century, rather than in the fourth century when Christianity became the official religion of the Roman Empire.

V. ABBREVIATIONS

The Attic inscriptions, in contrast to the Latin inscriptions, show in general but few abbreviations, most of them occurring in proper names and demotics.[58] The early Christian inscriptions from Athens use abbreviations sparingly. It is possible to distinguish two groups among them. Sacred names often appear with their first and last letters, or only with their initials.[59] In fact, the words Θεός, Ἰησοῦς, Κύριος, Χριστός are more often contracted than written out.[60]

The second group, more properly called abbreviations, contains words, the final syllables of which are omitted. The abbreviation is indicated by a line which intersects the last written letter, by a horizontal line above the last letter, or by the addition of a curved stroke resembling a Latin S.[61]

The most commonly abbreviated word is καί, often spelled κέ.[62] The earliest instance in Athens occurs in *I.G.*, II², 4513, dated for prosopographical reasons at the end of the second century after Christ. Next may be mentioned *I.G.*, II², 10934, dated in the third century after Christ, but probably a Christian tombstone (see above, note 31). All the other inscriptions containing this abbreviation for καί are definitely

---

[57] These new formulae are Κύριε βοήθει τοῦ δούλου σου – – –, and ἐκοιμήθη (or ἐτελειώθη) ἐν Κυρίῳ ὁ δοῦλος τοῦ θεοῦ – – – ; see W. M. Calder, *J.R.S.*, X, 1920, p. 55.

[58] See W. Larfeld, *Handbuch*, II, 2, pp. 515-537.

[59] See *I.G.*, III, 3475, 3534 (restore the first line as ✝ X M[Γ ✝] ; cf. W. K. Prentice, *Cl. Phil.*, IX, 1914, pp. 410-416), 3535, 3536, 3544; Konstantinides, Παρνασσός, VI, 1882, p. 81, no. 1 (Bayet, no. 10; see above, note 7) ; *Harmonia*, no. 1; Nos. 31 and 33.

[60] See M. Avi-Yonah, *Abbreviations in Greek Inscriptions*, *Quarterly of the Dep. of Ant. in Palestine*, Suppl. to Vol. IX, 1940, pp. 25-29.

[61] See Avi-Yonah, *op. cit.*, pp. 29-39.

[62] See Bilabel, *R.E.*, *s.v.* Siglae, cols. 2287 (lines 53-55), 2296 (lines 19-22), 2302 (lines 40-41) ; Avi-Yonah, *op. cit.*, pp. 73-74, *s.v.* καί.

Christian.[63] In one instance, at least, the syllable καὶ within the name Νίκαιος appears abbreviated.[64]

In this connection may be mentioned the ligature of omikron upsilon. This ligature is not an abbreviation, but its lack of occurrence among the pagan inscriptions may be significant.[65] Even on the early Christian inscriptions, this ligature is found but rarely.[66]

Special attention may be called to the abbreviations of the word κοιμητήριον which is so frequently used on the Attic stones. An unpublished epitaph from the Epigraphical Museum (E.M. 2200) contains the shortest form $\overline{KT}$, while another tombstone built into the East door of the Mount Lykabettos enclosure has κοιμ(ητήριον).[67] Finally, the inscription republished below as No. XXII shows the more complete and customary form κοιμητήρ(ιον).[68] In spite of its length, κοιμήτηριον was rarely abbreviated, but filled in its entirety the first line of about half of all the epitaphs on which it occurs; see Bees, op. cit., p. 38, note 2. If it was divided, either the last two syllables or the last syllable were written in a second line.

The other abbreviations which occur on the early Christian epitaphs from Athens can be easily paralleled from documents found elsewhere and dated in the fifth and later centuries.[69] Attention should also be called to the elision sign found in I.G., III, 1387.

It is tempting to use this examination of the abbreviations in order to arrive at approximate dates for the early Christian epitaphs of Athens. The lettering alone

[63] See I.G., III, 3444, 3451, 3459, 3524; Harmonia, no. 1; Ἀρχ. Ἐφ., 1914, p. 166, no. 5 (see above, note 14); Hesperia, IV, 1935, p. 186, no. 53 (= XI, 1942, p. 303, no. 62; see above, note 33); No. XII.

[64] See No. III; compare Avi-Yonah, op. cit., p. 23, notes 1 and 2.

[65] Larfeld, op. cit., II, 2, pp. 513-515, nos. 44-49, gives a good idea of how this ligature developed. We have been unable to find an example of Larfeld's no. 49 among the pagan texts. His reference to I.G., III, 14 = I.G., II², 1089 seems to be mistaken; see J. H. Oliver, Hesperia, X, 1941, pp. 82-83, no. 35, to which should be added an unpublished inscription from the Epigraphical Museum (E.M. 2891) which joins the two fragments illustrated by Oliver.

[66] See I.G., III, 3449, 3471, 3482, 3524; Harmonia, no. 7 (E.M. 678); Ἀρχ. Ἐφ., 1914, p. 166, no. 5 (see above, note 14); No. 5. In I.G., III, 3449, the ligature occurs at the ends of lines 3-5, and was obviously used only in order to have the lines end with complete words. The ligature itself is simply a regular omikron upon which a small upsilon is placed. We should like to add to this list I.G., III, 3446, assuming that the last letter of the first name is the ligature of omikron upsilon; the epitaph accordingly records the deaths of husband and wife, and not of two women; see above, notes 32 and 33.

[67] Lampakes, Δελτίον Χριστ. Ἀρχ. Ἑτ., II, 1894, p. 89, no. 2; cf. Kent, C.P., XLII, 1947, p. 64.

[68] An epitaph from Megara (Bayet, no. 115 = I.G., VII, 174), now in the Epigraphical Museum (E.M. 9953), reads κυμητή|ρ(ιον) followed by an abbreviation mark; the inscription begins and ends with a monogrammatic cross. The same abbreviation of κοιμητήριον is found on two stones from Corinth (C.G.-C.I., I, 1, nos. 46, 59).

[69] See I.G., III, 1387, 3497, 3509 (the abbreviations occur in lines 2-3: ἀναγν(ώστου); and 5: ἡμῶ(ν); compare p. 9), 3511; G. K. Zesios, Σύμμικτα, p. 13, note 1; No. XX; No. 5.

helps very little since the lunate forms of epsilon, sigma, and omega are widely used after the middle of the second century after Christ. On the Christian inscriptions, the lunate forms predominate except for a few instances of square epsilon, sigma, and omega.[70] The real change in the letter forms seems to occur in the seventh century, when the script becomes taller, narrower, and more " Gothic."

The abbreviations, too, abound in the later period; they show a further development of the types used in the earlier texts together with the addition of many new ligatures.

Among the few dated inscriptions of the fifth and early sixth centuries, mention may be made of an Attic text of *ca.* 410 A.D. (*I.G.*, II², 4225, illustrated by J. Kirchner, *Imagines*, plate 54, no. 151), of an inscription from Sardis dated in 459 A.D. (*Sardis*, VII, 1, no. 18 and plate VI), of an epitaph from Corinth, convincingly dated in 514 A.D. (*C.G.–C.I.*, I, 1, no. 41), and of a tombstone from Thessaly of *ca.* 540 A.D. (G. A. Soteriou, 'Αρχ. 'Εφ., 1929, p. 7, fig. 6). The two documents from the Isthmos which belong to the time of Justinian (*C.G.–C.I.*, I, 1, nos. 1 and 2) show few abbreviations; but the style of their lettering seems to us to be definitely later than that of the inscriptions with which we are dealing here. It is for this reason that we believe that the stones published and discussed here belong approximately to the fifth century after Christ.

VI. SYMBOLS

The great majority of the early Christian epitaphs from Athens are adorned with symbols, such as crosses of various shapes, monograms, rosettes, and representations of birds and leaves. It may be useful to describe these symbols here and to discuss the frequency of their occurrence and the position they occupy on the stones.

The appearance of a cross or a Christian monogram on a tombstone reveals to us that the burial it commemorates was that of a Christian. It may be doubted, however, whether the symbol was originally put there for that purpose. The pagan epitaphs from Athens are entirely free of any symbols referring to religious affiliations, and the use of the cross by the Christians (and of the seven-branched candlestick by the Jews) was evidently introduced from abroad. Most of the epitaphs which are considered Christian have crosses, but the occurrence of the word κοιμητήριον (or of a similar term; see above, p. 6), the use of the genitive of the name (see above, p. 6) and of καί (see above, p. 6), and the mention of clerical ranks (see above, pp. 8-9) have also been taken as evidence of Christianity. The fragmentary state of most of the tombstones and our lack of acquaintance with the originals do not permit us to state definitely that any Christian epitaph of Athens lacked a Christian symbol, but attention may be called to at least three stones which may belong to this category. Two of these (*I.G.*, III, 3518 and 3519) are of the simplest type, containing only the

[70] See *I.G.*, III, 3520; *Harmonia*, no. 12 (illustrated Plate VIII E.M. 9973); Nos. XXII, 3, 5.

names in the genitive. The third (*Hesperia*, VII, 1938, pp. 262-263, fig. 88) is very elaborate both in ornamentation and in the text of the inscription.[71]

The plain cross, in most instances consisting of two straight lines of equal length (Greek Cross), is found more often than any other Christian symbol. An examination of the more than two-hundred early Christian epitaphs from Attica reveals that this emblem occurs on more than one hundred stones. Very often the plain cross is placed at the beginning of the first line of the text, and it stands either inside or outside of the left margin of the inscription. On many stones the simple cross is found at the end of the last line.[72] It may be significant that in a number of completely preserved documents, the texts begin and end with simple crosses.[73]

On several stones, such crosses stand either above or below the inscription. Sometimes they stand alone, but in many instances they appear in groups of three.[74] This number may possibly have some relation to the Christian doctrine of the Holy Trinity. A Corinthian inscription (*C.G.–C.I.*, I, 1, no. 7), which contains two references to the Trinity, has three (?) crosses at the top, but only two at the bottom. Two epitaphs illustrated by G. A. Soteriou, Εὑρετήριον, I, p. 10, fig. 2, are crowned, one by three Constantinian crosses (see below, p. 16), and one by a swastika flanked by two plain crosses (see below, p. 17).

In addition to the plain crosses, we also find a larger and more decorative type of incised cross. On eight of the early Christian epitaphs from Athens, this emblem stands above the inscription and above the center of the first line.[75] On three monuments, two incised crosses are engraved above the text.[76]

[71] The first letters of lines 1-4 are missing and it may have been that a small and narrow cross was engraved at the beginning of the first or possibly the second line (see *C.G.–C.I.*, I, 1, no. 7, line 6). In fact, the second line, as restored now, would have had an uninscribed space in front of the name; we may, however, restore this name as [Εἰ]ουλλιανοῦ; see p. 20. The iota of τρ[ι]|άκοντα should be restored at the end of line 3.

[72] On two epitaphs (*I.G.*, III, 3485 and *Harmonia*, no. 7), where the last line is shorter than the others, this line is flanked by crosses.

[73] *I.G.*, III, 3436, 3456, 3474; *Harmonia*, no. 1; Nos. IV, XV, 8, and one unpublished epitaph of the Epigraphical Museum (E.M. 657).

[74] *I.G.*, III, 3443, 3459, 3465, 3470, 3525 (see below, p. 16 and note 85); J. Ch. Dragarses, Παρνασσός, VI, 1882, p. 252; *Harmonia*, no. 30 (now in the Epigraphical Museum, E.M. 9984); G. A. Soteriou, Εὑρετήριον, I, p. 56, fig. 43 (see below, p. 16); Nos. I and 25 (the third cross is restored); an unpublished epitaph of the Epigraphical Museum (E.M. 2228). On an inscription of only one line (*I.G.*, III, 3503), Bayet (no. 34) restored crosses at the beginning and the end of the text, and between the two words. On an epitaph from Megara (Bayet, no. 112), there are three crosses both above and below the text.

[75] *I.G.*, III, 3521, 3529, 3538; *Harmonia*, no. 21; P. Kastriotes, Ἀρχ. Ἐφ., 1914, p. 166, no. 4; O. Broneer, *Hesperia*, IV, 1935, p. 186, fig. 76 = XI, 1942, p. 103, no. 62; No. 19 (flanked by alpha and omega; see below, note 91); one unpublished epitaph of the Epigraphical Museum (E.M. 2225).

[76] *I.G.*, III, 3448; Nos. XVIII and XXI. According to Bayet (no. 36, plate I, no. 9) there is an incised cross also at the bottom of *I.G.*, III, 3448. Bayet states (no. 60, plate III, 4) that

On three tombstones, the large incised cross is enclosed within a circle,[77] and the same emblem (in two instances with the monogrammatic cross) is found on an architectural block from the Isthmos and on two epitaphs from Asia Minor.[78]

The incised cross often occurs on Attic tombstones flanked by two ornamental leaves, which together with the cross fill the width of the stone;[79] but this design does not seem to occur elsewhere. Even more peculiarly Attic is the replacement of the leaves by the first word (or part of it) of the inscription. In two instances, the cross stands in the middle of the first line (Nos. 6 and 16); it is of course larger than the letters and therefore extends above the line. On two stones, the cross intersects not only the first line but the first three or four lines of the inscription.[80] One short text (*I.G.*, III, 3463) is engraved all around the upper part of a very large incised cross; see also p. 22. Finally, there may be mentioned two epitaphs with long and elaborate inscriptions which are engraved on both sides of similarly large incised crosses (No. 15 and *Harmonia*, no. 12, Plate VIII E.M. 9973).[81] This arrangement of the text around a large cross or a similar symbol is found frequently in the later Byzantine period, and the origin of this custom may be traced back to the inscriptions mentioned here.[82] From this it may be gathered that epitaphs like No. 15 belong to a somewhat later period than the other Christian epitaphs discussed here.

A number of stones are decorated with monogrammatic crosses and Constantinian monograms.[83] The rhos used in these symbols are either of the open or of the closed type.[84]

there was a similar design below *I.G.*, III, 3460. In discussing the puzzling marks at the bottom of *I.G.*, III, 3451, he observes (no. 40 and plate II, 9): " Apparet ad quartam lineam tenue crucis vestigium." In *I.G.*, III, 3468, a pair of these crosses flank, according to Bayet (no. 19 and plate II, 11), the one line of the epitaph; see also No. X. A single incised cross stands at the beginning of the first line of *I.G.*, III, 3444; compare *C.G.-C.I.*, I, 1, no. 30.

[77] *Harmonia*, nos. 11 and 22 (Plate X E.M. 9981); No. 33. On *Harmonia*, no. 22 and no. 33, the emblem is flanked by two birds; see below, note 96.

[78] See *C.G.-C.I.*, I, 1, no. 4; *T.A.P.A.*, LVII, 1926, plates III, fig. 4, and IV, fig. 5.

[79] *I.G.*, III, 3439, 3454 (hitherto not noticed), 3466, 3475 (see below, note 86), 3493, Nos. VIII (see below, note 86) and 9. On *I.G.*, III, 3443, this design occurs below the text (possibly with a simple cross). Above the text of *I.G.*, III, 3516 there are preserved a leaf and the left arm of a simple cross (unnoticed by Bayet, no. 74 and plate IV, 14); the first line of the inscription contained more than the word τύνβ[ος], for the vertical bar of the cross (if the cross was placed symmetrically) probably stood above the last letter of this word.

[80] No. 11; G. A. Soteriou, Ἀρχ. Δελτ., II, 1916, p. 142, fig. 16. This latter epitaph was found on the north slope of the Areopagus and may, therefore, belong to the same cemetery as the stones from the Agora. If this should be the case, all but two epitaphs of this type belong to the same cemetery; see above, p. 3.

[81] On the front of *Harmonia*, no. 12, the names of the deceased were engraved within two large crosses; see below, p. 44.

[82] See *Harmonia*, nos. 37 and 38; Εὑρετήριον, I, p. 20, fig. 6 a; compare Ἐπετηρίς, VIII, 1931, pp. 244-246.

[83] See M. A. Frantz, *A.J.A.*, XXXIII, 1929, p. 10.

[84] See Frantz, *loc. cit.*, plate III, opposite p. 12.

The plain monogrammatic cross with the closed rho is found in *I.G.*, III, 3447, 3482, 3525,[85] 3531; *Harmonia*, no. 23; No. 29; on an unpublished epitaph of the Epigraphical Museum (E.M. 402). N. Platon has recently asserted ('Αρχ. 'Εφ., 1937, II, p. 666) that the usage of this symbol is confined to the second half of the fourth century and the beginning of the fifth. Simple monogrammatic crosses with the rho open and to the right are found on *Harmonia*, no. 7; G. A. Soteriou, Εὑρετήριον, I, p. 56, no. 43, and No. XXII. Two of the incised crosses which are flanked by leaves actually are in the shape of the monogrammatic cross of this type.[86] On three inscriptions, the open rho is to the left of the upper arm of the cross.[87] Two of these epitaphs are not completely preserved, and it is possible therefore, that the rho turned to the left was balanced by a rho turned to the right.[88]

The Constantinian monogram with the closed rho appears at the top of two epitaphs (*Harmonia*, no. 24 and No. VII), and on both inscriptions this symbol is flanked by alpha and omega.[89] The same monogram with the rho open occurs probably three times on a monument illustrated by G. A. Soteriou, Εὑρετήριον, I, p. 10, fig. 2. The central monogram is enclosed within a circle,[90] and the same ornament may be restored on *I.G.*, III, 3541.

The letters alpha and omega are found on seven of the early Christian epitaphs from Athens.[91] In two more inscriptions the order of these letters is reversed, with the possible meaning: "the end is the beginning." [92] Most peculiar, however, are the two epitaphs on which the letters occur apparently both in reversed order and upside down (*I.G.*, III, 3510 and No. III).

In discussing these various monograms, M. A. Frantz remarked (*loc. cit.*, p. 22) " that in Greece the use of the closed rho seems to be confined to private monuments, while the open rho is found in the pavement of the Byzantine Church of Hagios Georgios in Eretria, in the sculptures of the Asclepieum, as well as in other parts of Greece." On the Christian epitaphs from Athens, both open and closed rhos are found, not only in monogrammatic crosses, but also in Constantinian monograms.

---

[85] The central cross at the bottom of this inscription is drawn with double lines, which are filled out by cross lines, and it is flanked by omega and alpha; see below, note 92.

[86] *I.G.*, III, 3475 and No. VIII; compare *T.A.P.A.*, LVII, 1926, plate III, fig. 4; *C.G.–C.I.*, I, 1, no. 4.

[87] *I.G.*, III, 3484; No. 34; and an unpublished epitaph of the Epigraphical Museum (E.M. 2202).

[88] Compare the epitaph from Vienna illustrated by M. A. Frantz, *A.J.A.*, XXXIII, 1929, p. 13, fig. 2.

[89] For a discussion of alpha and omega, see below.

[90] For a similar design, see D. M. Robinson, *T.A.P.A.*, LVII, 1926, p. 203, no. 12 and plate VII, fig. 12.

[91] Bayet, no. 60; *I.G.*, III, 1386, 3489, 3536; *Harmonia*, no. 12 (see Plate VIII E.M. 9973); Nos. VII and 19.

[92] *I.G.*, III, 3525 and *Harmonia*, no. 22 (see Plate X E.M. 9981); compare Swoboda, Keil and Knoll, *Denkmäler aus Lykaonien*, p. 21, no. 32, and *M.A.M.A.*, I, no. 324.

The swastika is found only once, so far as we know, on a Christian epitaph from Athens.[93] The design stands at the top of the inscription, and it is flanked by two crosses (see above, p. 14). This ancient oriental symbol occurs frequently on Christian monuments of a small region of Pisidia, Lycaonia, and Isauria.[94]

The rosette, a favorite Greek ornament, is found at the bottom of No. III, and in the gable of the Jewish epitaph, I.G., III, 3545. This ornament occurs more frequently in decorative art and on inscriptions of the Byzantine period.[95]

Some Christian epitaphs from Attica are adorned with representations of birds. In two instances, a pair of birds flank an incised Greek cross.[96] The design may be compared with the central part of the relief from Ravenna, illustrated by G. W. Elderkin, Kantharos, plate VIII (opposite p. 41). At the bottom of another inscription (No. X), two birds stand on either side of a vessel from which a branch extends. The same design is found on a somewhat later Attic relief; see A. Orlandos, Εὑρετήριον, III, p. 197, fig. 262. On the inscription published in Hesperia, VII, 1938, pp. 262-263, fig. 88, a single bird is represented "pecking at a large leaf" (Broneer), but this leaf may actually be a rough drawing of a vessel.

Both on the Attic relief (Εὑρετήριον, III, p. 197, fig. 262) and on the relief from Ravenna (Elderkin, op. cit., plate VIII), branches with grapes grow out of a crater.[97] It is interesting, therefore, to find the representation of a bunch of grapes at the lower right corner of an early Christian epitaph from Athens (I.G., III, 3525).

Incised leaves appear frequently on Attic inscriptions, both pagan and Christian, of this period.[98] The incised cross flanked by two leaves is a favorite design which occurs not only at the top of a great number of Attic epitaphs (see notes 77 and 84) but also as an architectural ornament.[99] There is an elaborate floral design below the text of I.G., III, 3523, and the inscription of I.G., III, 3544 is flanked by two leaves. Two closely joined leaves stand at the top of I.G., III, 3484.

On the Jewish epitaphs from Athens, the seven-branched candlestick replaces the

[93] See G. A. Soteriou, Εὑρετήριον, I, p. 10, fig. 2. The significance of the hole near the bottom of the front face of this stone is discussed by G. A. Soteriou, Byz.-Neugr. Jahrb., X, 1933-1934, p. 179. The swastika was also used as an ornament for an early Christian church of Athens; see A. Xyngopoulos, Ἀρχ. Ἐφ., 1915, p. 58, fig. 9.

[94] See A. M. Ramsay, J.H.S., XXIV, 1904, pp. 260-292; Aberdeen Univ. Studies, XX, 1906, p. 33.

[95] See Harmonia, no. 36, and Εὑρετήριον, I, p. 20, fig. 6 a, and p. 58, fig. 45.

[96] Harmonia, no. 22 (Plate X E.M. 9981) and No. 33.

[97] Compare also M.A.M.A., VI, plate XXVIII, no. 160.

[98] Single leaves are found below the last line of two inscriptions (I.G., III, 3537 and No. XIII) and at the end of the last line of eight others (I.G., III, 3510, 3527; Harmonia, nos. 11 [= E.M. 9999] and 29 [= E.M. 9978]; Ἀρχ. Δελτ., II, 1916, p. 142; Hesperia, VII, 1938, pp. 262-263, fig. 88; Nos. VII and XX). The leaf at the bottom of No. XXI was probably balanced by another at the right.

[99] See, for example, Εὑρετήριον, I, p. 38, fig. 20; M.A.M.A., VI, plate 68, no. 386.

cross. In addition to the stones already recognized as Jewish,[100] we may list *I.G.*, III, 3596, which shows traces of the base of a seven-branched candlestick above the inscription.[101] The same symbol is found at the bottom of another Attic epitaph (*I.G.*, II², 10949), which Kirchner recognized as Jewish.

Only one of these Jewish stones has any additional symbols. On *I.G.*, III, 3546, there is incised to the left of the candlestick a trumpet and to the right a palm tree.[102]

VII. SPELLING AND PRONUNCIATION

A change in spelling, or a consistent and widespread misspelling, may be taken as an indication of a change or shift in pronunciation. This general rule is confirmed by the peculiar spellings found among the early Christian inscriptions from Athens.

It is now commonly assumed that from about 150 A.D. " the pronunciation of αι as ε became established in the speech of the educated people." [103] Among the Christian inscriptions, which belong, for the most part, to the fifth century, we counted 35 occurrences of the spelling καί, compared with only 20 of the more phonetic spelling κέ. This should be taken as evidence that the " correct " spelling of καί was well known in early Christian times. On the other hand, there are six examples of κῖτε (for κεῖται) and two of κῖμε (for κεῖμαι), compared with one occurrence each of κεῖται (*I.G.*, II², 13216 B = Bayet, no. 42; Christian? see p. 10), κῖται (*I.G.*, III, 3525), and κεῖμαι (*I.G.*, III, 3527).[104]

Final -αι, both in the infinitive and in the third person singular, is written as epsilon in six instances.[105] Mention may also be made of the phonetic spellings which occur in *I.G.*, III, 3536 and in Nos. XV and XXIII, but in all these cases the number of examples is too small to allow generalizations. It may be significant, however, that the name Ἀθήναιος is spelled Ἀθήνεος in all three instances in which it occurs.[106]

[100] *I.G.*, III, 3545 and 3546 = *C.I.I.*, I, 712 and 713; see above, note 30. Compare also *Antioch*, II, p. 150, no. 24.

[101] Compare W. M. Ramsay, *Cities and Bishoprics of Phrygia*, II, p. 651, no. 561; W. H. Buckler and W. M. Calder, *M.A.M.A.*, VI, p. 119, no. 347.

[102] This epitaph was included in the *Corpus Inscriptionum Iudaicarum*, I (no. 713) by P. J.-B. Frey, but the trumpet at the left is mistakenly represented in the illustration as another palm tree. Representations of trumpets, candlesticks, and palm trees are often found on Jewish epitaphs; see *C.I.I.*, I, nos. 200, 283, 343, 374, 382, 416, 479, 499, 519, 523, 600, 646, 647, 648, 652, 657, 671. For the representation of a palm tree on a Christian epitaph, see *M.A.M.A.*, VI, plate 39, no. 221.

[103] E. Sturtevant, *Pronunciation*, p. 142; compare the evidence presented by K. Meisterhans, *Grammatik*³, pp. 34-35; W. K. Prentice, *Greek and Latin Inscriptions* (1908), p. 350 (Orthographical and Grammatical Index); H. J. Leon, *T.A.P.A.*, LVII, 1927, pp. 210-233; P. Chantraine, *The Link*, I, 1938, pp. 7-10.

[104] See also below, the discussion of itacism, pp. 18-20.

[105] Two of these occur on *I.G.*, II², 13216 C (Bayet, no. 42), and we wonder whether this inscription (C) is part of the same epitaph as *I.G.*, II², 13216 B which contains the " correct " spelling κεῖται (see above, p. 10).

[106] *I.G.*, III, 3454, 3545, No. X; compare *C.G.–C.I.*, I, 1, no. 46.

As should be expected, αι is mistakenly written instead of ε in several inscriptions which are mentioned by Meisterhans (see above, note 103); to these may be added Nos. I and VII of this publication. Rather peculiar are three inscriptions in which epsilon or alpha iota apparently replaced iota or an equivalent vowel.[107]

The confusion of the vowels ει, η, ι, οι and υ, commonly called itacism, is of a much later date than the documents with which we are dealing, and this fact is clearly shown by the evidence presented here.

The word κοιμητήριον which occurs so often on the Christian epitaphs from Athens is correctly spelled on 32 inscriptions while the spelling with upsilon instead of omikron iota occurs on 36 stones.[108] This again shows that the " correct " spelling was well remembered by the Christian Athenians of the fifth century. It seems significant that the two etas in κοιμητήριον or κυμητήριον were only rarely replaced by iotas.[109]

In addition to the substitution of upsilon for omikron iota found in the spelling of κοιμητήριον, there are four instances in which various forms of the verb ἀνοίγω (for classical ἀνοίγνυμι) are spelled with upsilon,[110] and one example of the spelling ὑκητήριον (I.G., III, 3504). On the other hand, there is but one case in which omikron iota is written instead of upsilon.[111]

It is not surprising that there are very few instances in which iota (or eta) was written instead of upsilon (or omikron iota).[112] In two inscriptions upsilon stands for iota (or eta).[113]

It is a well-known fact that the diphthong ει was equated and confused with iota long before the beginning of our era.[114] This statement is borne out by the evidence collected from the Christian epitaphs. There are eleven examples of the spelling κῖτε (κῖται, κῖμε, κατάκιτε, κατοικῖ), but only one of κεῖμαι (I.G., III, 3527).[115] Many other words which occur only once or twice show the same shift in spelling.[116] The change from eta to iota occurred later and does not seem to be as well established by the fifth

---

[107] I.G., III, 3459 (πενακᾶ may be the genitive of a noun πενακᾶς meaning " maker of πίνακες "; see above, p. 8), 3533; I.G., II², 13224 (see above, p. 10), No. 31.

[108] See Sturtevant, op. cit., p. 146; Meisterhans, op. cit., p. 59, note 502.

[109] See below, p. 20. Aside from the inscriptions in which the word is incompletely preserved, we noticed only one example of κοιμιτίριον (I.G., III, 3473), three of κυμητίριον, and five of κυμιτίριον; see also No. 18.

[110] I.G., III, 1428; I.G., II², 13216 C; Harmonia, no. 1; G. K. Zesios, Σύμμικτα, p. 13, note 1.

[111] I.G., III, 3436; see Meisterhans, op. cit., p. 59.

[112] See the spellings μιλιναρίου (G. Lampakes, Δελτ. τῆς Χριστ. Ἀρχ. Ἑτ., I, 1892, p. 67) and Βηζάντιος (I.G., III, 3483). A Megarian inscription (Bayet, no. 114, apparently not reprinted in I.G., VII) has the doubtful spelling κιμιτήριον; compare No. XIV.

[113] See No. 15. An unpublished epitaph in the Epigraphical Museum (E.M. 403) contains the word [μ]υστύριον.

[114] See Meisterhans, op. cit., pp. 48-56; Sturtevant, op. cit., pp. 129-131.

[115] For I.G., II², 13216 B, see note 105.

[116] ι for ει: S. A. Koumanoudes, Ἀθήναιον, IX, 1880, p. 171, no. 2; G. Lampakes, Δελτ. τῆς Χριστ. Ἀρχ. Ἑτ., I, 1892, p. 67. ìς for εἰς: G. K. Zesios, Σύμμικτα, p. 13, note 1. For other examples, see I.G., III, 3457, 3535; Bayet, no. 114 (Megara); Harmonia, no. 1; Nos. IX and 5.

century. We have already noticed (see note 109) that the two etas in κοιμητήριον or κυμητήριον were but rarely replaced by iotas,[117] and the other instances of this substitution are both small in number and occur in unusual words.[118] On the other hand, there are quite a few examples of the reverse substitution of epsilon iota and of eta for iota, but none of them is in any way unusual.[119]

A few words may be added concerning a small number of peculiar usages of the vowels, omikron, omikron upsilon, upsilon, and omega. Most of these can be explained by similar occurrences which have already been noted. In No. 15, τιμωρίαν is spelled τιμουρίαν, and the same substitution occurs in an unpublished text (E.M. 2221: ὑδραγούγου).[120] In the same No. 15, we read χρούσινα for χρύσινα, and this change, too, is found elsewhere.[121] Omega and omikron are confused in several domuments.[122] In one inscription (No. II) Σώλου is written for Σαύλου, and this spelling may be compared with that of Σωφήιος for Saufeius (*I.G.*, II², 3897). The change from omikron to epsilon, which is found in two instances,[123] has been noticed elsewhere.[124]

In the use of consonants we have noticed particularly the change from lambda to rho which occurs too frequently to be a mere mistake.[125] In five inscriptions double consonants are written with a single letter,[126] and in one epitaph we read ['I]ουλλιανοῦ (*Hesperia*, VII, 1938, pp. 262-263) instead of ['I]ουλιανοῦ; see also note 71.

Among the peculiarities in declension, there is only one which is significant enough to deserve a detailed discussion. Both Bayet and Meisterhans have already noted [127] that several proper names (and at least one noun) ending in -ης have their genitive in -η instead of -ου. The same observation has been made also by N. Bees who collected (*C.G.–C.I.*, I, 1, p. 111; see also pp. 76, 78, 79, 112) the various occur-

[117] We counted only nine examples.

[118] For σηρικάριος we read once σιρικάριος (*I.G.*, III, 3513) and once σιρηκάριος (Εὑρετήριον, I, p. 10, fig. 2). The name Εὐφήμιος (or Εὐφημία) is misspelled twice (*I.G.*, III, 3445 and 3455), and Δημήτριος once (*I.G.*, III, 3476 = Bayet, no. 70; the reading should be Διμητρί[---]). ἔχη is spelled twice ἔχι (Bayet, no. 106; No. IX) and we found once the spelling γαμικῖς for γαμικῆς (*I.G.*, III, 3483). Compare E. Nachmanson, *Eranos*, XXXVIII, 1940, pp. 108-109, 118.

[119] ει for ι: Bayet, no. 10 (see note 7); *I.G.*, III, 1387, 3436, 3458, 3527; No. XX. ει for η: *I.G.*, III, 3504. η for ι: *I.G.*, III, 3459, 3509; G. K. Zesios, Σύμμικτα, p. 13, note 1; Εὑρετήριον, I, p. 10, fig. 10 (*bis*). η for ει: *I.G.*, III, 3459; *I.G.*, II², 13216 C = Bayet, no. 42.

[120] See E. Schwyzer, *Grammatik*, p. 185, Zusatz 1. The genitive [Πε]ρικλέως is found on *I.G.*, III, 3520.

[121] See *I.G.*, II², 13224 (compare notes 51 and 125) and Meisterhans, *op. cit.*, p. 30, note 155.

[122] See Meisterhans, *op. cit.*, pp. 24-25, note 128.

[123] No. VII and *Hesperia*, VII, 1938, pp. 262-263.

[124] See Meisterhans, *op. cit.*, pp. 22-23; Schwyzer, *op. cit.*, pp. 354-355.

[125] To the collection of Meisterhans, *op. cit.*, p. 83, note 713, may be added *I.G.*, III, 3486 (Φλεβουαρίῳ), G. Lampakes, Δελτ. τῆς Χριστ. Ἀρχ. Ἑτ., II, 1894, p. 89 (χαρκέως; see above, note 40), G. K. Zesios, Σύμμικτα, p. 13, note 1 (τορμήσῃ). The various peculiarities in spelling which appear in *I.G.*, II², 13224 tend to confirm our assumption that this is a Christian epitaph (see note 51).

[126] *I.G.*, III, 3443, 3449 (see below, note 131), 3458 (see below, note 133); Nos. IX and 9.

[127] *De Titulis*, p. 66, in the commentary on no. 2; *op. cit.*, p. 120, no. 9.

rences of the genitive Ἀνδρέα and Ἀνδρέου. An explanation of this irregularity was offered by E. Schwyzer (*op. cit.*, p. 561) who stated that these genitives were derived according to the rule " Gen. = Nom. minus *s*."

The Attic epitaphs which we have examined supply the following evidence in support of these general observations.

The regular form Ἀνδρέου occurs not only on *I.G.*, III, 3449 and *Harmonia*, no. 10 (E.M. 9972),[128] but also on Nos. 4 and 5. The genitive Ἀνδρέα, on the other hand, is found not only on *I.G.*, III, 3456,[129] but also on No. 3 and in three unpublished inscriptions in the Epigraphical Museum (E.M. 402, 2221, 3425 + 4753). It also occurs in the epitaph published by G. A. Soteriou, Ἀρχ. Δελτ., II, 1916, p. 142, fig. 16.[130] The same form of the name should be restored in *I.G.*, III, 3515,[131] and, possibly, in 3473.[132]

The name Ioannes which occurs on the Attic epitaphs almost as frequently as Andreas has also two forms for the genitive (Ἰωάννου, Ἰωάννη), corresponding exactly to Ἀνδρέου and Ἀνδρέα. The regular form Ἰωάννου is found on *I.G.*, III, 3449,[133] 3458, 3486, 3503, 3505.[134] 3535; No. XVII. The form Ἰωάννη, on the other hand, occurs on only two inscriptions (Bayet, no. 10 [see note 7]; No. 9), but the use of this genitive form is also confirmed by the genitives Ἐπιφάνη (*I.G.*, III, 3459), Ἑρμῆ (*I.G.*, III, 3519),[135] Θεοκράτη (S. A. Koumanoudes, Ἀθήναιον, IX, 1880, p. 171, no. 2), Πασικράτη (*I.G.*, III, 3464) and οἰκαίτη (No. VI).[136]

Faulty forms are rare among the Christian epitaphs from Athens. We noticed only the dative μελλόντοις (*Harmonia*, no. 1) for μέλλουσι.

VIII. GUIDE LINES

Many of the Attic Christian inscriptions are cut between thin guide lines. It is obvious that these lines were drawn across the face of the stone before the inscription was engraved. Such guide lines are well known from the Attic dedicatory and funer-

---

[128] These two Attic examples are mentioned by Bees who also listed two texts (*I.G.*, III, 3480 and 3516) in which the name is incompletely preserved and the genitive ending cannot be restored with certainty.

[129] This is the only Attic text listed by Bees.

[130] The second line of this inscription should be restored as [Ἀν]δρέα μικ[ροῦ]; compare *I.G.*, III, 3486, and F. Preisigke, *Wörterbuch*, *s. v.* μικρός.

[131] The second and third lines are apparently a later addition, and the whole text should be restored as [τό]πος Ἐλπι[δίας (?)] | καὶ Ἀν[δ]|ρέα. It seems that Elpidia died before her husband; see also note 32.

[132] An examination of the squeeze shows that only one letter is missing in the third line, but this space may have been filled by the ligature of omikron and upsilon; see above, note 66.

[133] The name is completely preserved and is spelled Ἰωάν|ου; see above, note 126.

[134] The restoration of lines 2-3 as [Ἰω]ά[ν]νου is possible, but uncertain.

[135] The inscription may read Ἑρμῆ καὶ Φιλίν(ν)ας.

[136] See Meisterhans, *op. cit.*, p. 120, note 101.

ary inscriptions of the sixth and early fifth centuries before Christ.[137] No special investigation of the occurrence of these guide lines among the later Attic inscriptions seems to have been made thus far, and a few examples taken from the early Christian documents may, therefore, be listed and discussed here.

The guide lines which occur on *I.G.*, III, 3462, 3463 and VII, 170-171 have been illustrated in the *Corpus* and by Bayet (plate II, 1 and plate IV, 2). In *I.G.*, III, 3462, the guide lines are *ca.* 0.034 m. apart, and the inscription is neatly engraved between these lines. In *I.G.*, III, 3463, the stonecutter not only drew thin guide lines (also 0.034 m. apart), but he also drew thin lines which guided him in the engraving of the large incised cross; compare also E.M. 9973 illustrated on Plate VIII. It appears, moreover, that the cross of *I.G.*, III, 3463 was cut before the inscription was engraved, but after the guide lines for the inscription were drawn. This is made clear by the fact that lines 1 and 4 were engraved with little regard for the guide lines, but with respect to the already incised cross; see above, p. 15.

In addition to the examples already mentioned, eleven more of the early Christian epitaphs from Athens show the use of guide lines.[138] The two preserved guide lines of *I.G.*, III, 3476 are *ca.* 0.027 m. apart, and they stand above and below the second line of the text. In *I.G.*, III, 3488, there is a set of two guide lines (*ca.* 0.017 m. apart) drawn *ca.* 0.02 m. below the inscription, the letters of which are *ca.* 0.024 m. high. It seems that these guide lines have never been used.[139] In *I.G.*, III, 3492, there are four guide lines, *ca.* 0.021 m. apart. One thin line intersects the first line of the text, slanting upward to the right. It seems that the stonecutter drew this line first and then abandoned it. The inscription of *I.G.*, III, 3534 is engraved between guide lines which are 0.034 m. apart; this is noteworthy because the same distance between guide lines has been observed on *I.G.*, III, 3462, 3463, and on No. 26 of this publication. On *Harmonia*, no. 11 there are three guide lines; the second is *ca.* 0.037 m. below the first, and the third is *ca.* 0.031 m. below the second. The five guide lines which appear on a Jewish inscription from Athens (*I.G.*, III, 3545) are *ca.* 0.025 m. apart.

IX. SHAPE OF THE STONES

In addition to borrowing many of the old pagan formulae for their epitaphs, the Christians of Athens also used the same types of monument. Most of the Christian

---

[137] See W. Larfeld, *Handbuch*, I, pp. 204-205 (Richtlinien); *Griech. Epigraphik*, p. 130; A. Rehm, *Handbuch der Archäologie*, I, p. 216, note 2; A. E. Raubitschek, *J.H.S.*, LX, 1940, pp. 58-59; W. Peek, *Kerameikos*, III, p. 21 and plate 7.

[138] *I.G.*, III, 3476, 3488, 3492, 3534; *Harmonia*, nos. 11 and 22 (Plate X E.M. 9981); Nos. XIV, XXI, XXIII, 21, 26, 27, and 30; compare also the Jewish inscription, *I.G.*, III, 3545.

[139] Similarly in *C.G.–C.I.*, I, 1, no. 44, the inscription is engraved between pairs of thin guide lines (*ca.* 0.018 m. apart, with an intermediary distance of *ca.* 0.009 m.), which also cover the uninscribed lower portion of the stone, as has been noticed by A. N. Skias, Ἐφ. Ἀρχ., 1893, col. 127, no. 22; see above, note 11.

inscriptions are engraved on thin stone plaques, commonly called *cippi*.[140] These plaques were well known in pagan times, and a fine example is illustrated by J. Kirchner, *Antike*, XV, 1939, p. 95, fig. 11. In order to make clear the frequency of the use of plaques for Christian graves, a list of the known examples may be given here.[141]

Besides these comparatively thin *cippi*, thicker stones, or pillars, were also used. The monuments included in this group vary in height, and their thickness is always more than one third of their width; some of them are almost square. This shape of stone was used less frequently than the plaques; a list of the known examples is given below.[142]

A number of Christian epitaphs are engraved on small columns, the so-called *columellae* or κιονίσκοι. The early history of this type of grave monument has been outlined by J. Kirchner, *Antike*, XV, 1939, pp. 94-95. The examples from the Christian period show both the continuity of the ancient form, and its acceptance by the members of the new faith. The known examples are listed below.[143]

The Christians of Athens not only copied the style of the pagan monuments, but, in several instances, they used for their own epitaphs stones which had once marked the graves of pagans. The columnar grave monuments published below (Nos. 8 and 12) are good examples of this reuse. The pagan inscriptions of these epitaphs were engraved *ca.* 100 B.C.; thus more than five-hundred years passed before the stones were reused. A survey of the Christian epitaphs from Athens reveals that several others are engraved on stones which had been used previously, perhaps as tombstones.[144] Only one Christian tombstone (*I.G.*, III, 3521) was reused to serve again

[140] This word indicates the simplest type of *lapis sepulcralis*. Apparently the use of *cippi* in ancient times was not affected by the legislation of Demetrios in 317 B.C., for they are not mentioned by Cicero in his account of that law (*De Legibus*, II, 26), and we have, of course, many examples of *cippi* which date both before and after that year. For a further discussion on the law of Demetrios, see *Hesperia*, XII, 1943, pp. 144-165; *A.J.A.*, XLVIII, 1944, p. 239, note 16.

[141] *Harmonia*, nos. 1, 7, 12 (Plate VIII E.M. 9973), 14, 18 + 33 + E.M. 9975 (see above, note 12), 22 (Plate X E.M. 9981), 23, 25, 27, 28, 29, 30, 32, 34; Nos. XII, XV, XVIII, XX (Christian?), XXI, XXII, XXIII, 3, 4, 5, 7, 9, 10 (reused, see below, note 145), 11, 14, 15, 16, 17, 18, 19, 20 (reused, see below, note 145), 21, 22, 23, 24, 25, 26 (reused, see below, note 145), 27 (reused, see below, note 145), 29, 30 (reused, see below, note 145), 31, 33, 34. Neither Bayet nor Dittenberger recorded the thickness of the stones which they published, and none of them is therefore listed here; see notes 142 and 143.

[142] *Harmonia*, nos. 11, 21, 24; *Hesperia*, IV, 1935, p. 186, no. 53; VII, 1938, pp. 262-263; XIII, 1944, pp. 252-253, no. 19; Nos. VII, XIII, XIV, XVII, 1, 2, 6, 28 (reused, see below, note 145). For the omission of the inscriptions published by Bayet and Dittenberger, see notes 141 and 143.

[143] *I.G.*, III, 3441, 3460, 3465, 3474, 3506, 3518, 3523, 3527; Ἀρχ. Ἐφ., 1914, p. 166, no. 4; *I.G.*, II², 11782, 12825, 13216 (reused, see below, note 144); Nos. 8 (reused, see below, note 144), 12 (reused, see below, note 144) and 13. Dittenberger's terminology (*columna, columna rotunda, columella rotunda*) is sometimes misleading.

[144] In addition to the columnar grave monuments mentioned above (Nos. 8 and 12), here may be listed *I.G.*, III, 3445, 3453; *I.G.*, II², 3283 *c*, 7119 (see above, note 31), 13216 (columnar grave

for a Christian grave (*I.G.*, III, 3522). Several other Christian monuments had been previously used as architectural blocks, or as marble roof tiles.[145]

Several Christian epitaphs are engraved on stones which are sometimes called *basis*, sometimes *epistylium*.[146] It may be that this group of monuments should be classified as *mensae* or *τράπεζαι*; see J. Kirchner, *loc. cit.*, p. 95.

X. THE CORPUS INSCRIPTIONUM GRAECARUM CHRISTIANARUM

In spite of the great interest in the early history of Eastern Christianity, the *Corpus Inscriptionum Graecarum Christianarum* has made little progress since the work was so auspiciously announced by Théophile Homolle (*B.C.H.*, XXII, 1898, pp. 410-415; compare Bees, *op. cit.*, pp. viii-ix). The publication of the Christian inscriptions from Egypt and Asia Minor deserves special mention, but the mainland of Greece and the Greek islands have been greatly neglected.[147] Quite recently, Johannes Kirchner announced in the preface of *I.G.*, II², pars tertia, fasciculus posterior (1940), p. 5: Titulos sepulcrales Christianos in Attica repertos, quos G. Dittenberger operi suo inseruit, ab hac sylloge abalienavimus. Christianas inscriptiones, quotquot prodierunt, Johanne Lietzmann et Georgio Soteriu moderantibus opere peculiare editum iri sciendum est. The first fascicule of the *Corpus der Griechisch-Christlichen Inschriften von Hellas* (abbreviated: *C.G.–C.I.*), edited by N. A. Bees and comprising about half of the inscriptions from the Isthmos and from Corinth, appeared in 1941. In the preface (p. ix) Bees announced that the documents from Attica and Salamis are to be published as the third volume of this series. In the meantime, we may be permitted to offer some corrections of inscriptions already published, and to present most of the early Christian texts which were found during the Agora excavations. We wish to thank Professor Henri Grégoire for help in the interpretation of some of the more difficult of these. Professor William K. Prentice offered many valuable corrections and suggestions. We are also grateful to Professors Harald Ingholt and George Soteriou who kindly read the manuscript.

XI. COMMENTS ON THE PUBLISHED TEXTS

In the following account a discussion of some already known inscriptions (Roman numerals) precedes the publication of the recently found documents from the Agora (Arabic numerals).

monument, see above, note 143); 'Αρχ. 'Εφ., 1925-1926, p. 97, fig. 2 (engraved on the back of *I.G.*, II², 1806 *a*; see above, notes 16 and 41) and No. VII.

[145] *Hesperia*, XIII, 1944, p. 265, no. 19; Nos. 10 (plaque, see above, note 141), 26 (plaque, see above, note 141), 27 (plaque, see above, note 141), 28 (pillar, see above, note 142), 30 (plaque, see above, note 141) and 32; see also note 18.

[146] *I.G.*, III, 3452, 3456, 3457 (= *I.G.*, II², 13240; double tombstone), 3468, 3503, 3520 (*in parte sarcophagi*), 3524 (?), 3534 (?), 3535 (?), 3536 (?) and No. V (double tombstone).

[147] See the useful bibliographical summary given by Jalabert and Mouterde, in Cabrol-Leclercq, *Dictionnaire d'Archéologie Chrétienne*, VII, 1, cols. 624-625 and 692-693.

I (Plate I). *I.G.*, III, 3437 should be joined to *I.G.*, III, 3481 *b*. Fragment *a* (*I.G.*, III, 3437) is part of a plaque of Pentelic marble; place and date of discovery are unknown. The fragment is now in the Epigraphical Museum (E.M. 9870). To the bibliography given in *Inscriptiones Graecae* there may be added Bayet, no. 51, and plate 4, no. 8. Fragment *b* (*I.G.*, III, 3481 *b*), a fragment of Pentelic marble, of unknown provenience, is also in the Epigraphical Museum (E.M. 2252), and was also published by Bayet, no. 55.

Frag. *a*   Frag. *b*

Κοιμη[τ]ήριο[ν]
Εὐτύχου
[καὶ] Ἀλαι
ξ[ά]νδρας.
† † [†]

Fragment *b* was originally combined with the fragment now published as *I.G.*, III, 3481 *a*. This combination was made by Bayet (*B.C.H.*, II, 1878, p. 164, note 1), who based his suggestion on a copy of Fragment *b* which he found in his notebook. A comparison of the squeezes of *I.G.*, III, 3481 *a*, 3481 *b*, and 3437 clearly shows that *I.G.*, III, 3481 *b* joins *I.G.*, III, 3437 and has nothing to do with *I.G.*, III, 3481 *a*.

The original width of the plaque may be estimated by a study of the crosses which appear at the bottom. The cross below the delta in line 4 seems to indicate the center of the front face. The distance from the center of this cross to the left edge is *ca.* 0.16 m., and the total width of the plaque was therefore *ca.* 0.32 m.

The restoration of *I.G.*, III, 3481, line 4 (Θεο[δώ]ρας) has now to be abandoned, and the restoration of *I.G.*, III, 3437, lines 3 and 4 (Ἀλ[ε]ξ[αν]δ[ρ — — —]) must be modified. Traces of a letter seem to be preserved in front of the delta in line 4, and this letter may have been a nu although the preserved stroke, if it belonged to a letter at all, looks more like

the top of an epsilon. Judging from the other Christian tombstones, it should be assumed that the two names of this inscription were connected by καί (possibly spelled κέ), and this conjunction may be restored at the beginning of line 3. This would necessitate the restoration of a woman's name Ἀλαιξ[ά]νδρα in lines 3 and 4.[148]

II. A photograph of the inscription published as *I.G.*, III, 3438 (= Bayet, no. 66), which is now kept in the Byzantine Museum, is illustrated by G. A. Soteriou, Εὑρετήριον, I, p. 10, fig. 2; *Guide*[2], p. 43. From this illustration it appears clearly that the reading first made by Koumanoudes (*op. cit.*, no. 3604: Μαρτυρίου) and the restorations suggested by Bayet (Μαρτυρί[ου], Μαρτυρίο[υ]), as well as the new reading (?) by Soteriou (*Guide*[2], p. 42: Μάρτυρος) are all incorrect. The last partially preserved letter of the third line was an alpha, a lambda, an upsilon, or a chi. It is clear that the only reasonable restoration can be:

† Κοιμητήρ[ιον]
Σώλου
Μαρτυρίᾳ[ς].

It must be noticed, however, that in most of the Attic Christian funeral inscriptions containing two names, the names are connected by καί; see above, note 31. For the spelling of the name Σώλου, see above, p. 20.

III (Plate I). *I.G.*, III, 3465 is a columnar grave monument of Hymettian marble, found in the Theatre of Dionysos, and now in the Epigraphical Museum (E.M. 9898); it was published also by Bayet, no. 8.

[∀] ω
[†] † †
[Κοι]μητή
[ριο]ν Νικ(αί)ου.

The inverted omega at the top was probably preceded by an inverted alpha; see above, p. 16. For the rosette, see above, p. 17. All the previous editors have restored the name in line 2

---

[148] The occurrence of αι for ε is peculiar but well attested for this period; see above, p. 19.

as [E]ὐνίκου; such a reconstruction is incorrect. The first preserved letter of the second line is not an upsilon but a nu; the letter immediately above is a mu. If the three letters KOI (and not KY as in *I.G.*, III, 3465) are restored in the first line, the same number should be restored below. The preserved vertical stroke of the first extant letter in line 2 is therefore part of the final nu of the word [κοι]μητή[ριο]ν. The name that follows begins with a nu and may be read as Νικ(αί)ου.

This reading is suggested by the peculiar form of the kappa with a tail, a form which in many other instances is used as an abbreviation for καί.[149]

IV (Plate I). *I.G.*, III, 3487 was first published by Bayet, no. 83; the stone is now in the Epigraphical Museum (E.M. 9915).

> † Κvμητ[ήρι]
> ov Τυχι[κοῦ]
> καὶ Εὐφη[μί]
> [ας]. †

Both Bayet and Dittenberger assumed that the inscription was written in three lines, with a cross below the center of the third line. It is clear, however, from the illustration, that the cross was not placed in the center, but at the end of the last name, which extended into a fourth line. Bayet was right in assuming that this epitaph recorded the burial of a man and his wife; see above, pp. 6-7.

V (Plate I). *I.G.*, III, 3502 was first published by Koumanoudes, *op. cit.*, no. 3580, and his publication was the sole basis for the text as printed in *Inscriptiones Graecae* and in Bayet, no. 37. The stone is now in the Epigraphical Museum (E.M. 9944).

a	*b*
[Κοιμητ]ήριον	Κοιμη[τήριον]
[—³⁻⁴—]ης κὲ Καλ	Ἀλέξω[νος].
[—²⁻³— ο]υς.	

This base of Hymettian marble contains two inscriptions, apparently written by two different hands. Koumanoudes, who failed to record the first line of the second inscription (*b*), considered all as one text and read the second line as IC κὲ Καλῦς Αλεξ.ω..... An examination of the squeeze reveals traces of the word κοιμη[τήριον], beginning above the first letter of the name Ἀλέξω[νος] and obviously belonging to this name. Since it is unlikely that the word κοιμητήριον was repeated in the same inscription, and since the texts marked as *a* and *b* seem to be engraved by different hands, it may be assumed that two Christian epitaphs were engraved on the same stone.[150]

Inscription *a* consists of the word [κοιμη-τ]ήριον (in one line) and two names, connected by κέ. The first name, the end of which was read by Koumanoudes as IC, was that of a woman and it ended in [———]ης (genitive).[151] Assuming that this name began underneath the kappa of [κοιμητ]ήριον, the restoration [Ἀγάπ]ης would fill the space.

The second name begins with the letters ΚΑΛ after which Koumanoudes read ΥC. No traces of these last two letters are visible on the squeeze, and it is unlikely that they ever stood there since the last preserved letter lambda stands underneath the last letter of [κοιμη-τ]ήριον, thus probably marking the end of the line. On the other hand, there seem to be traces of two letters of a third line preserved, and these may be the two letters read by Koumanoudes as ΥC The second of these letters (the last of the inscription, since it is followed by an uninscribed space) is certainly a sigma, as the alternative reading (epsilon) is not a genitive ending. The letter before the sigma may well have been an upsilon, but only the top of the right slanting stroke is preserved.

Inscription *b* consists of the word κοιμη-[τήριον] followed by one name. This is indicated by the uninscribed space below the second

---

[149] See above, pp. 11-12; compare M. Avi-Yonah, *Abbreviations in Greek Inscriptions*, p. 23, notes 1 and 2.

[150] For a discussion of double tombstones, see above, p. 7.

[151] For this unusual arrangement, see above, note 32.

line. In the engraving of the name Ἀλέξω[νος], the stonecutter first used an artistic form of the letter xi, and later inserted the more common form immediately after the epsilon; see, however, P. Graindor, *B.C.H.*, XXXVIII, 1914, p. 289, note 1.

VI (Plate I). *I.G.*, III, 3513 was first published by Koumanoudes, *op. cit.*, no. 3553, and was republished by Bayet, no. 102. The stone was found, according to Koumanoudes, in the Attic village Trachones, and it may therefore have once stood in the cemetery of the early Christian church found in this region (G. A. Soteriou, Ἀρχ. Ἐφ., 1929, p. 195; A. Orlandos, Εὑρετήριον, III, pp. 155-156); it is now in the Epigraphical Museum (E.M. 9932).

> † Μνημόριον Διο-
> νυσίου σιρικαρί-
> ου οἰκαίτη τοῦ
> λαμπροτάτου
> 5 Πλουτάρχου ἀν-
> θυπάτου.

The significance of this epitaph lies in the fact that it mentions one of the governors of Greece, the proconsul Ploutarchos. Various attempts have been made to identify the proconsul with other bearers of the name Ploutarchos; they have all failed because they were based on the assumption that three other inscriptions, two from Athens (*I.G.*, II², 3818 and 4224) and one from Megara (*I.G.*, VII, 94-95), all refer to the same person. The σοφιστής Ploutarchos, who erected *ca.* 410 A.D. a statue of the prefect Herkoulios (*I.G.*, II², 4224), called himself μύθων ταμίης, and is praised by the Athenians as βασιλεὺς λόγων and σταθερῆς ἕρμα σαοφροσύνης (*I.G.*, II², 3818). He may be no other than the famous philosopher Ploutarchos, the son of Nestorios, father of Hierios, grandfather of another Ploutarchos, and teacher of Proklos.[152]

The Ploutarchos, however, who was honored in the Megarian inscription (*I.G.*, VII, 94-95) evidently was not a man of letters. He is called a descendant of proconsuls and prefects (ἀπ' ἀνθυπάτων καὶ ὑπάρχων), and he is praised on account of his justice (καθαρῆσιν ἀοίδιμον εὐνο-μίησιν; πάντῃ δ' εὐνομίης εὖχος ἀπειρέσιον; πολλῶν ἀντ' ἀγαθῶν ἀμφὶ Δίκης τεμένει). It is evident that this man held a public office connected with the administration of justice. We are tempted, therefore, to identify him with the proconsul Ploutarchos whom we know from the Athenian inscription. Unfortunately, neither the Athenian nor the Megarian inscription can be accurately dated. We know the names of four, possibly of five, proconsuls of Greece who held office during the last thirty years of the fourth century (*I.G.*, II², 4222, 4223, 4226, 5205; Kaibel, *Epigrammata Graeca*, no. 918 [?]). It may be that Ploutarchos should be added to this list.[153] We do not know whether or not Ploutarchos was an Athenian. The fact that his slave Dionysios was buried near Athens can hardly be used as evidence.

Two more Athenians of this period with the name Ploutarchos are known (*I.G.*, II², 12473; *I.G.*, IV², 436-437); neither of these seems to have any connection with the proconsul.

The occupation of Dionysios is given as σιρικάριος; see above, p. 8 and note 118. For the spelling of the word οἰκαίτη, see above, note 103.

VII (Plate II). *I.G.*, III, 3516 a was first published by Koumanoudes, Ἀθήναιον, VI, 1877, pp. 384-385, no. 7.

> Α ⳨ ω
> Τύμβον ὃν εἰσ-
> ορᾷς Ζωσιμιανῆς
> ὦ ξέναι
> ♂ φιλέγονε
> 5 σώφρων.

[152] See R. Hirzel, *Plutarch*, p. 77, note 9; K. Praechter, *Byz. Zeitschr.*, XXI, pp. 426-430; A. von Premerstein, *Jahreshefte*, XV, 1912, p. 32, note 110; G. Rodenwaldt, *Griechische Porträts*, p. 13, note 18; P. Graindor, *Chronologie*, p. 288, note 1.

[153] This observation is confirmed by L. Robert (*per ep.*) who dates Ploutarchos in the reign of Constans; cf. Hanton, *Byzantion*, IV, 1927/8, pp. 64-65; Groag, *Diss. Pann.*, XIV, 1946, pp. 59 ff.

Koumanoudes reported that the ends of lines 3 and 4 were mutilated, but it is clear from the illustration that the last 3 lines of this inscription, although shorter than the first two, are completely preserved. The strokes above the final letters of line 4, which may possibly form a nu, belong to an earlier inscription of which faint traces are visible all over the inscribed surface; see above, note 144. We assume that this stone marked the grave of a young child, for the epitaph is addressed to any visitor (compare Lattimore, *op. cit.*, pp. 230-234, no. 63) who loves children (for the spellings ξέναι and φιλέγονε, see above, p. 19 and note 123). The word σώφρων may be taken as another vocative (following φιλέγονε), or as the predicate. In the latter case, one may wonder whether the fourth line should not read φίλε γόνε (a hybrid imperative form of γίγνομαι). For a discussion of the symbol above this epitaph, see above, p. 16; for a discussion of the leaf, see above, note 98.

VIII (Plate II). *I.G.*, III, 3517 was first published by Bayet, no. 23; the stone is now in the Epigraphical Museum (E.M. 9936). We illustrate the inscribed part here in order to call attention to the monogram.

ℛ ✝ ℛ

Κυριακοῦ.

Dittenberger has already indicated the heavy lines above and below the name, and the leaves which flank the cross; see above, note 79. He did not, however, call attention to the fact that the cross is rendered in the form of *crux monogrammatica* with the open rho; see above, note 86. A monogram of exactly the same type appears on a coptic stele from Egypt.[154]

IX (Plate II). The stone with the inscription now published as *I.G.*, II², 13222, was found in the Theatre of Dionysos, thus in a region where many Christian tombstones were discovered and where apparently a Christian cemetery was located. Moreover, an examination of the squeeze reveals traces of a cross below the letters ΞΗ of the next to the last line of the inscription. It is clear, therefore, that this fragment was once part of a Christian epitaph, and the text of the inscription, if properly restored, confirms this assumption.

The restoration of the text as suggested by Koumanoudes (*op. cit.*, no. 3873 = *I.G.*, III, 1426) is not acceptable because it requires too many letters to be supplied at the end of the third line. Judging from the necessary restorations in lines 4 and 5, four letters at the most are missing after ταύτην in line 3. It may be noticed, incidentally, that Koumanoudes saw more of lines 4 and 5 than seems to be preserved today. Peek's reading (*I.G.*, II², 13222) of the first word of the third line (θῖναι = θεῖναι) is an improvement, but his interpretation of the following word ΕΧΙ (presumably for ἔχοι; see *I.G.*, II², 13213, line 6) as ΕΙΣ is wrong. The inscription may be confidently restored as follows.

[—⁶⁻⁷—] ἤν [τις τολ]
μή[σ]ει τινὰ ἄλλ[ον]
θῖναι, ἔχι ταύτην [τὴν ἀ]
ράν· μήτε γῆ μή[τε θά]
5 λασα δέξη αὐ[τοῦ τὰ]
ὀστᾶ.

✝

Instead of an uninscribed space after ἄλλ[ον], in line 2, there may have been [ισ]θῖναι; compare, however, *I.G.*, II², 13211, line 2: εἰ δέ τις ἔτερον τολμήσει θεῖναί τινα. The restoration of the end of the third line [τὴν ἀ]ράν is one letter too long; it may be that one should restore [τίν] rather than [τήν]. The reading and restoration of the first line are too uncertain to justify any comment. For the phrase ἔχοι ταύτην τὴν ἀράν, reference may be made to a considerably later document from Thessaly containing the curse ἔχι τὴν ἀράν τῶ(ν) ἁγίω(ν) π(α-

---

154 See M. A. Frantz, *A.J.A.*, XXXIII, 1929, p. 23, figure 6; compare C. Bonner, *Proc. Am. Philos. Society*, LXXXV, 1941, p. 90, fig. 7.

τέ)ρ(ων).[155] For the use of the word ἀρά, see the examples quoted below (in the commentary on No. XII) ; see also *I.G.*, VII, 2183 and *I.G.*, II², 13188, lines 15-16. The mention of land and sea is unique in this formulation, but a similar phrase occurs in *I.G.*, II², 13209, line 9 = 13210, lines 14-16: μὴ γῆ βατὴ μὴ θάλασσα πλωτή; compare Lattimore, *op. cit.*, pp. 114-115; Bees, *op. cit.*, p. 33. For the curse directed against the bones of a possible violator, see below, No. XII.

X. The inscription published by Bayet, no. 11, has not found its way into *Inscriptiones Graecae.* The stone was found near the sanctuary of Asklepios, on the South Slope of the Akropolis, and it is now in the Byzantine Museum.[156] The photograph published by Soteriou (see note 156) permits a complete restoration of the text.

[†] Κυμη †
τήριον
['Ἀ]θηνέου.

It is clear that the ornament at the bottom indicates the middle of the inscribed face. We must assume, therefore, that the large cross in the right upper corner was balanced by a similar cross in the upper left corner, and that the second line of the inscription began somewhat farther to the left than the first line; see note 76. The third line would then have started even more to the left, its first letter standing underneath the foot of the cross. The restoration of the text suggested above is based on this observation.

For a discussion of the design at the bottom of this epitaph, see above, p. 17; for the spelling of the name Athenaios, see above, note 106.

XI (Plate III). The inscription published by Bayet, no. 13, has not found its way into *Inscriptiones Graecae.* It was discovered in the sanctuary of Asklepios, and is now in the Epigraphical Museum (E.M. 4258). The stone is broken only at the top. Height, 0.15 m.; width, 0.15 m.; thickness, 0.08 m. M. Mitsos kindly supplied us with a description of the stone.

[τ]ὸν Ἅ
γιον 'Ἀ
νδρέαν.

Bayet was probably correct in reading the name 'Ἀ|νδρέαν in lines 2 and 3, for the marks after the alpha of line 2 do not seem to belong to a letter. He did not notice, however, the faint traces of a gamma at the beginning of the second line. Lines 2 and 3 are, therefore, completely preserved, and only one letter is missing at the beginning of the first line.

The name Andreas occurs more frequently on the Attic Christian tombstones than any other name.[157] This may be due to the fact that Andreas is not only a good Greek name, but also the name of one of the Apostles, who preached the Gospel in Greece, and who, according to tradition, suffered martyrdom at Patras in Achaia.

The text of this inscription differs, however, from the others because the name is in the accusative. It is known that an early Christian church stood in the old sanctuary of Asklepios, and it is possible, therefore, that this inscription records the dedication of a statue, or even of the church itself, in honor of Saint Andrew.[158]

---

[155] See N. I. Giannopoulos, Ἐπετηρίς, XII, 1936, p. 404, no. 6; compare W. M. Ramsay, *Luke the Physician*, p. 397, note 1. For the curse of the 318 Fathers who assembled at the Nicene Council, see M. Holleaux, *B.C.H.*, IX, 1885, p. 83, no. 13; W. M. Ramsay, *Cities and Bishoprics of Phrygia*, II, p. 555, no. 429; De Waele, *op. cit.*, pp. 40-41. The phrase νὰ ἔχῃ τὰς ἀρὰς τῶν ἁγίων πατέρων is found as late as 1548; see Δελτ. τῆς Χριστ. Ἀρχ. Ἑτ., I, 1892, pp. 138-139, no. 12.

[156] See G. A. Soteriou, Εὑρετήριον, I, p. 10, fig. 2; *Guide²*, p. 43.

[157] It is frequently found also on the Christian epitaphs from Corinth; see De Waele and Bees, *op. cit.*, p. 65.

[158] See M. Lambert, *B.C.H.*, I, 1877, pp. 169-170, and plates VII-VIII; A. Xyngopoulos,

XII (Plate II). The inscription published by Bayet, no. 79, has not been included in *Inscriptiones Graecae*, but it was republished, without reference to Bayet, by K. M. Konstantopoulos, *Harmonia*, no. 2. Both Bayet and Konstantopoulos copied the text in the Museum of the Archaeological Society. The stone is now in the Epigraphical Museum (E.M. 9967). It is a plaque of white marble, broken above, below, and at the right. Its preserved thickness is, according to Konstantopoulos, 0.04 m.

> Μαρτυρίου
> κ(αὶ) Μαρτυρίας·
> εἴ τις δὲ τολ
> μήσει κατε
> περάνω κατ[ά]
> ρα κ(αὶ) πανάρ[α]
> τοῖς ὀστοῖ[ς].

The name Μαρτύριος is well attested for the early Christian period.[159] On the other hand, the name Μαρτυρία seems to be otherwise unknown. It has been suggested above (No. II) that this name be restored in another Attic inscription. For the abbreviation of καί, see above, note 61.

Bayet printed in his text only the first three lines and part of the fourth, stating " post verbum τολμήσει nihil intellexi certum; haec autem, sed timide, conjici posse videntur; καθάπερ ἄνω κατάρᾳ καὶ παναβύσσοις. . . ." Konstantopoulos, on the other hand, gives a complete and intelligible text except for the last two lines. It seems clear that the last three lines of the inscription should be read as printed above, meaning " an all-out curse on his bones." [160] The preceding phrase, εἴ τις τολμήσει κατεπεράνω, although its significance is clear, contains the puzzling word κατεπεράνω. It may be suggested that this is a combination of κατεπάνω (found in medieval and modern Greek) and ὑπεράνω, and not a substitute for καθυπεράνω, as Konstantopoulos suggests. The curse in this inscription seems to be unique; it is similar, however, to that contained in another Attic inscription which is now published among the pagan tombstones (*I.G.*, II², 13222), but which is in fact a Christian epitaph (see above No. IX).

Attention should be called to the peculiar shape of the nu and rho of line 6; compare the letters of the inscription discussed on p. 9.

XIII (Plate II). The inscription published by Bayet, no. 81, is not in *Inscriptiones Graecae*, but it was republished, without reference to Bayet, by Konstantopoulos, *Harmonia*, no. 19. The text was copied both by Bayet and by Konstantopoulos in the Museum of the Archaeological Society, and the stone is now in the Epigraphical Museum (E.M. 9979). Konstantopoulos reports that part of the top is preserved, and that the original thickness is 0.095 m., while the width is only 0.16 m.; see above, note 142.

> Ἡ τὴ[ν μα]
> καρία[ν]
> μνήμη[ν]
> Ἀνικητία
> 5   ἐνθάδε
> κατοικῖ.
> ⳨

Ἀρχ. Ἐφ., 1915, pp. 52-71; G. A. Soteriou, Εὑρετήριον, I, pp. 46-47. Xyngopoulos discusses the remains of several Christian churches, and dates the first at the end of the fifth century (*loc. cit.*, p. 53). For an early representation of Saint Andrew, see Δελτ. τῆς Χριστ. Ἀρχ. Ἑτ., I, 1892, p. 131, no. 13, and plate I.

[159] See *R.E.*, *s. v.* Martyrios; Jalabert and Mouterde in *Dictionnaire d'Archéologie Chrétienne*, VII, 1, col. 636, note 12.

[160] A good parallel for this curse is found in a pagan inscription from Crete: ἐπάρα κατάρα κακὴ τῷ ἀσεβήσαντι – – – ; see *Inscriptiones Creticae*, I, p. 207, no. 64; compare also the phrase ἐξώλης καὶ πανώλης (J. Merkel, *Über die Sogenannten Sepulcralmulten*, pp. 22-23; *S.E.G.*, VI, 802, line 19; *C.G.–C.I.*, I, 1, no. 15) and ἐπικατάρατος (*I.G.*, XII, Supplement [1939], p. 196, no. 1179; W. M. Ramsay, *Cities and Bishoprics of Phrygia*, II, p. 559, no. 445).

Bayet's text contains only lines 3-6 (probably because he was unable to restore the beginning; compare No. XII), but the text given by Konstantopoulos is both correct and complete. The phrase ἡ τὴ[ν μα]καρία[ν] μνήμη[ν] occurs in the same position on several Christian epitaphs from Corinth.[161] It may be presumed that this phrase was in common use in Corinth while it was only rarely employed in Athens; compare Bees, *op. cit.*, pp. 39-40. In fact, it is by no means certain that this epitaph originally stood in Athens.[162] The phrase ἐνθάδε κατοικῖ is a variation of the pagan κεῖται or κατάκειται, adapted to the Christian usage. As Konstantopoulos observed, κατοικῖ (for the spelling, see p. 19) may be compared with οἰκητήριον and κατοικητήριον; see *I.G.*, II², 12825, recognized by Bayet (no. 43) as a Christian tombstone.

Attention may be called to the occurrence of the " Latin " delta (see below, note 179) and to the leaf below the inscription (see above, note 98).

XIV (Plate III). The inscription published by Bayet, no. 87, is not published in *Inscriptiones Graecae*, but it was republished, without reference to Bayet, by Konstantopoulos, *Harmonia*, no. 31. The stone was copied both by Bayet and by Konstantopoulos in the Museum of the Archaeological Society. It is now in the Epigraphical Museum (E.M. 9982). Attention may be called to the thickness of the stone, which is recorded by Konstantopoulos as 0.15 m.; see above, note 142.

Κυμη[τήριον Εὐ]
γένου[ς καὶ Σωτ]
ήρα[ς].

The unusual thickness of the stone, considered with the small size of the lettering, may

indicate that only a little of each of the three lines is preserved. The restoration as suggested above differs from that given by Bayet and Konstantopoulos, since it tries to give the first and second lines equal length. As to the restoration of the proper names, Bayet's statement may be repeated: nomina incerta sunt.

The second letter of the first line is an upsilon (Konstantopoulos) and not an iota, as Bayet has it; enough of the letter is preserved to show the fork of the two slanting strokes.

The three lines of the inscription are engraved between carelessly drawn guide lines; see above, note 138.

XV (Plate III). The inscription published by Bayet, no. 95, has not found its way into *Inscriptiones Graecae*, but it was republished, without reference to Bayet, by Konstantopoulos, *Harmonia*, no. 20. The stone is now in the Epigraphical Museum (E.M. 9988).

†

† Κυμιτίριον
Ἰσιδώρου
ἀναγνώστου
μαχερᾶ. †

Bayet reports, " lapis servatus dicitur ἐν τῷ ὑπουργείῳ ἐκπαιδεύσεως, sed negavit Eustratiadis antiquitatum, ut multi iam experti sunt, haud urbanus ephorus. Apographum communicavit benevolentissimus Koumanoudes." In spite of these difficulties, the text published by Bayet is correct. Attention may be called, however, to the fact that the inscription is engraved in four lines (and not in two as Bayet has it), that there are crosses above, in front of, and at the end of the text, and that the spelling of the first word is κυμιτίριον (and not κοιμητήριον as Bayet prints it). Konstantopoulos' text is

---

[161] *I.G.*, IV, 408; *Corinth*, VIII, 1, nos. 147, 151, 153; *C.G.–C.I.*, I, 1, nos. 17, 31, 33, 55, 56; see also Soteriou, *Guide¹*, p. 21; *Guide²*, p. 42.

[162] In discussing ὁ or ἡ τὴν μακαρίαν μνήμην, Konstantopoulos stated (*Harmonia*, p. 29, in the commentary on no. 17; see above, note 11) that this phrase does not occur on Attic inscriptions, referring in particular to the epitaph of Aniketia which he published as no. 19. It should be noticed, however, that this inscription is not included by Bees in his collection of the texts from Corinth (*C.G.–C.I.*, I, 1).

correct in all these respects; he fails, however, to give any dimensions.

The fourth line of the inscription offers some difficulty. Bayet (*De Titulis*, Index, p. 128) seems to take Μαχερᾶ as the genitive of the name Μαχαιρᾶς, and this name is indeed attested.[163] It would be puzzling, however, to find recorded here the deaths of two men whose names are not even connected by the usual καί.[164] Konstantopoulos offered the suggestion that Μαχέρα (not Μαχερᾶ) was the surname of the reader Isidoros.[165] It should be noted, however, that the original meaning of μαχαιρᾶς is " cutler." [166] It is quite conceivable that Isidoros, the cutler, also served as reader in his church.[167]

Attention should be called to the four thin guide lines, which appear in the illustration. They are 0.029-0.030 m. apart and very neatly drawn; see above, note 136.

XVI (Plate III). The inscription published by Konstantinides, Παρνασσός, VI, 1882, p. 84, no. 11, is now in the Epigraphical Museum (E.M. 5675).

ЄΝЄΝΚЄ

ΤΟΝΚΥΡΙΝ

Konstantinides' transcription is correct, but his restored reading (Ἐνέγκατε τῷ κυρίῳ [δόξαν καὶ τιμήν]) is not in keeping with his own text. The uninscribed space at the left apparently indicates that we have the beginning of two lines, and the raised band at the right makes

it clear that the inscription did not continue to the right. The same impression is gained from the peculiar spelling of Κύριον in the second line, obviously due to the engraver's desire to write the complete word in the available space.

We assume, with some hesitation, that ENENKE is the infinitive ἐνέγκαι which was part of a phrase like εἰ δέ τις τολμήσει ἕτερόν τινα νεκρὸν ἐπεισενέγκαι, or something similar. The second line τὸν Κύριον may be completed with the words κεχολωμένον ἕξει or similar. Both phrases are common enough in Asia Minor, but it should be noticed that they have τὸν Θεόν instead of τὸν Κύριον.

The large size of the letters (*ca.* 0.035 m.) may indicate that only a small fragment of a large monument is preserved.

XVII (Plate III). The inscription published by Konstantopoulos in *Harmonia*, no. 3, is now in the Epigraphical Museum (E.M. 9966). The stone was found below the Northeast Slope of the Akropolis, near the Church of the Anargyroi.

†

† Κυμητήριον

Ἰωά⟨ν⟩νου κα

ὶ Ἐνεχλίας.

The stonecutter apparently forgot to complete the first nu of the name Ἰωάννου. If that letter were completed, it would resemble the peculiarly shaped nu found in line 6 of the inscription published above, No. XII. Konstantopoulos reads the second name as ⟨Γ⟩ενε-

---

[163] Josephus, *Ant. Jud.*, XIV, 434-438 (15, 7); *Bell. Jud.*, I, 317-327 (16, 6-17, 2); compare L. Robert, *Rev. de Phil.*, XVIII, 1944, p. 41, note 4.

[164] See, however, notes 31 and 33.

[165] The peculiar separation of the name and surname by the title may be paralleled in English by the similar use of the title Canon or Cardinal: e. g., John Canon Smith, or John Cardinal Smith.

[166] The word is used today in this sense, and it apparently had the same meaning in earlier times; see *Ox. Pap.*, XIV, pp. 134-135, no. 1676, line 6; L. Robert, *Rev. de Phil.*, XVIII, 1944, p. 52, note 4; for the spelling with epsilon instead of alpha iota, see above, p. 18.

[167] Compare, e. g., F. Halbherr, *A.J.A.*, XI, 1896, pp. 608-609, no. 6: Ἰωάνν[ης] ἀν(αγνώστης?) κ(αὶ) χαρτουλάρ[ιος]; E. Hanton, *Byzantion*, IV, 1927-1928, p. 74: Ἰωάννης ὁ εὐλαβέστατος διάκονος καὶ ἰητρός; C. Wessel, *Inscr. Gr. Christianae veteres Occidentis*, p. 25, no. 145: Διονυσίου ἰατροῦ πρεσβυτέρου; G. Bakalakis, Θρακικά, VIII, 1937, no. 6 (reported in *R.E.G.*, LII, 1939, p. 477, no. 188, 6): Παύλ(ου) πρεσβ(υτέρου) καὶ ζωγράφου.

χλίας (for Γενεθλίας). This interpretation may have been influenced by the occurrence of the name Γενεθλία[s] in the immediately following inscription (no. 4 of Konstantopoulos' article, republished here as No. XVIII). Bees (*op. cit.*, p. 117) accepted this reading and called attention to the phonetic significance of the change from gamma to iota (and from theta to chi ?). It seems more probable, however, that the first letter of line 3 is the final iota of the conjunction καί, part of which is written in line 2.[168]

The name Ἐνέχλια, unique at least in this spelling, may be derived from the verb ἐνοχλέω (which has a bad connotation), or from a combination of ἐν and ὄχλος (comparable to Ἔνδημος). It is also possible that the name is a derivative of the Attic place name Ἐχελίδαι which, at least in one instance, is referred to as Ἐνεχελιδῶ (*Et. Mag.*, *s. v.*). The final sigma of the genitive ending is smaller than the other letters, and is written somewhat above the line. The upper stroke of this letter is extended to the right.

XVIII (Plate IV). The inscription published by Konstantopoulos, *Harmonia*, no. 4, is now in the Epigraphical Museum (E.M. 9968).

$$† \quad [†]$$

Οἰκητή[ριον]
τῆς μα[καρίας]
καὶ ἀειμ[νήστου]
καὶ ἀλησ[μονήτου]
5 Γενεθλία[s μοναχῆς (?)].

The incised cross at the left was probably balanced by another at the right; see above, note 76. Lines 2-4 contain a series of adjectives and not names, beginning with the word τῆς (line 2) and connected by καί (lines 3 and 4). The restoration suggested by Konstantopoulos for line 4 (ἀλήσ[του] accepted by Bees, *op. cit.*, p. 117) is too short, and ἀλησ[μονήτου], which is found on another Christian epitaph (*I.G.*,

III, 3446) is preferable. Since the letters of the last line appear to be more closely spaced, it may be that the name Γενεθλία was followed by another word which completely filled the fifth line. The restorations suggested for lines 2-5 require a length of line longer than that of the first, and it seems possible, therefore, that the last words of these lines may have been abbreviated.

XIX (Plate IV). The inscription published by Konstantopoulos, *Harmonia*, no. 5, is now in the Epigraphical Museum (E.M. 49). A fragment in the same museum (our squeeze has no inventory number) probably joins above, and another (E.M. 3508) joins below. These three fragments belong, according to Konstantopoulos' description of the one he published, to a triangular pillar of Pentelic marble. The front face and the adjoining right side of the middle piece are 0.24 m. wide, while the left side measures 0.23 m. The front face of the fragment which joins above is only *ca.* 0.235 m. wide (measured on the squeeze), and it seems possible that the pillar tapered toward the top. The front face of the lower fragment is not completely preserved; the right side of this fragment is inscribed. The piece published by Konstantopoulos was found at the intersection of the ὁδοί Ἑρμοῦ and Νορμάννου, near the place where the early Christian Church of St. Agathokleia stood (see below, note 180). In spite of that coincidence, this epitaph is not Christian; see above, p. 10. It is known, moreover, that other pagan inscriptions were found in the same locality; see below, note 182.

a

[------]
[*ca.* 5 ἐν ταύ]
[τ]ηι τῆι ἐ[ντομί]
δι ἥτις ἔχει
5 βάθους ὀρυγ
σομέ[νη τ]άσδε
ἄλλας καὶ τὴν

b

ΠΟ[---]
ΡΙΝΙΣ[---]
ἐτελ[ειώθη ---]
ΛΙΚΟ[---]

---

[168] Compare the division of κ|αί in *I.G.*, III, 3508.

σορὸν τοῖς ἐ
μοῖς. Εἰ δέ τις
10 [‒ca. 3‒] κεινήσει
[τι τὴν] θήκην εἰ⟨ς(?)⟩
[τὴν ἐντο]μίδα τῶ[ι]
[ἱεροτάτωι τα]
[μείωι ‒‒‒‒]

The inscription may have begun with the name of the deceased and the phrase ἐνθάδε κεῖμαι. The relative pronoun in line 4 (ἥτις) introduces the verb ἔχει, which governs the accusatives in lines 6-8: " which contains (holds) these other coffins and my own casket." In the phrase τὴν σορὸν τοῖς ἐμοῖς, the word ὀστοῖς is of course understood: " for my bones." [169] The feminine form ὀρυσσομέ[νη] is required both by the length of the lacuna in line 6 and by the relative pronoun ἥτις, with which it agrees; it is modified by the genitive βάθους: " being dug in depth " or " deeply cut." This restoration and interpretation assumes that ἥτις (line 4) refers to the underground chamber or excavated vault in which the remains of several persons were kept, and we have restored the word ἐντομίς both in lines 3 and 12 because it has this meaning. L. Robert (*Études Épigraphiques et Philologiques*, pp. 219-221) referred to several examples of the use of this word in epitaphs, and he maintained that it signifies a tomb that has been excavated or dug; the term seems to have been used primarily in Macedonia. It is interesting to note Hesychios' definition ἐντομίδας· μαμιλάρι (*leg.* σμιλάρια), ψαλίδια. The word ψαλίδιον is the diminutive form of ψαλίς, the primary meaning of which is " scissors "; it also means " vault " or " crypt," and thus confirms Robert's interpretation of ἐντομίς.[170] The reading and restoration of the first part of line 3 agrees with the remains of the seven vertical strokes, except that the iota of τῆι stands a little too far from the preceding eta (the cross stroke of which is preserved).

In line 9, the punctuation mark between ἐμοῖς and εἰ indicates the beginning of a new sentence; the traces are faint, but there is clearly an uninscribed space between these two words. This new sentence expresses a threat directed against possible violators of the tomb, and it begins with the customary phrase εἰ δέ τις, followed by some compound of the verb κεινήσει in line 10.[171] The restoration of lines 11-12 is uncertain, and even the meaning of the passage is not clear. According to the text suggested here εἰ⟨ς⟩ [τὴν ἐντο]μίδα would mean " in the vault," εἰς being used instead of classical ἐν with the dative. In front of θήκην one may prefer to restore ἄλλην. In that case, the meaning would be " move another casket into the vault." All these restorations presuppose that at the end of line 11 a sigma has been omitted. It should be mentioned, however, that the letters ΕΙ may stand for the particle ἤ.

The imprecation probably imposed a fine on anyone who might violate the tomb, and the last preserved word in line 12 (τῶ[ι]) makes it possible to restore in the following lines ἱεροτάτωι ταμείωι δώσει, or a similar phrase. It should be noted that in most instances the verb δώσει is placed first, but in *I.G.*, II², 13209 and 13224 the dative comes first.

We are unable to suggest any restoration for the four partially preserved lines of the right side; the third line may possibly have contained some form of the verb τελειόω.

Konstantopoulos has already seen that line 9 contains the beginning of a threat directed against a possible violator of the tomb. He apparently thought, however, that the use of this formula indicated that the document is Christian. Yet, in the preserved part of the inscription, there is no indication of Christianity, and the letter forms clearly show that the tombstone belongs to the second or to the early part of the third century after Christ.

---

[169] The term σορός occurs also in *I.G.*, II², 13211.

[170] For the use of ψαλίς in this meaning, see the dictionaries and W. K. Prentice, *Greek and Latin Inscriptions* (1908), pp. 126-127, no. 110.

[171] The verb μετακεινήσει occurs in similar documents (*I.G.*, II², 13209, 13210 and No. XX), but it has there a different meaning.

This text should therefore have been included among the *Tituli sepulcrales cum diris et poenarum sanctionibus*, B. *Monumenta reliqua*, *I.G.*, II², 13209-13228.

XX (Plate IV). The inscription published by Konstantopoulos, *Harmonia*, no. 6, is now in the Epigraphical Museum (E.M. 9969). Another fragment, published as *I.G.*, II², 13219 (see above, p. 10), joins at the bottom, thus completing the document. It should be noticed, however, that the thickness of the upper part, as reported by Konstantopoulos, is 0.035 m., while that of the lower part, as given by Kirchner, is 0.05 m. The width of the stele, as measured on the squeeze along line 7 of the joined fragments, is *ca.* 0.265 m.

> Ἐνταῦ[θα]
> κεῖται Φ[λ(άβιος)]
> Μαιωρῖνο[ς]
> νουμ(έρου) Ἐρούλ
> 5 ων. τούτου ὃς
> ἂν βουληθ⟨ε⟩ῖ μετα
> κεινῆσαί τι τῆς θήκ(ης)
> ἢ ἕτερόν τινα κατα
> θέσθαι, δώσει τῷ
> 10 ἱερῷ ταμείῳ ἀργύρου
> λείτρας δύο. ⳩

Konstantopoulos noticed that the letters of the first two lines are bigger and more widely spaced, but his restoration is made without regard to this observation. Since the width of the stone is now known, the restoration of line 1 must be ἐνταῦ[θα] because the missing fragment was at this point *ca.* 0.085 m. wide. In line 2, the name Φλάβιος must have been abbreviated (only *ca.* 0.075 m. of this line is missing), but the abbreviation may have been Φ[λ(άβιος)] or Φ[λά(βιος)]. In line 3, after Μαιωρῖνο[ς], there was a space of *ca.* 0.045 m. This space

may have been uninscribed, or it may have been filled by [ἐκ] | νουμ(έρου) which would correspond to the Latin *de numero*.[172] In line 4, the space after the lambda was *ca.* 0.05 m. If this space was uninscribed, as we assume, lines 2-4 would have had about the same length, while lines 1 and 5 would have been only slightly longer. In this case, the uninscribed space at the end of all these lines may have been filled by a Christian monogram. This means that Konstantopoulos' restoration of lines 5-6 (τούτου ὅσ[τις] ἂν βουληθ⟨ε⟩ίη) must also be changed, and in fact the normal formulation of this phrase is ὃς ἄν (with the frequent addition of δέ), and not ὅστις ἄν; βουληθ⟨ε⟩ῖ stands for βουληθῇ (W. K. Prentice). At any rate, it is extremely unlikely that Νουμέρου was the name of Maiorinos' father, unless it was misspelled for Νουμερ(ί)ου. The only other restoration of line 4 may be νουμέρου Λ[$\overset{ca.\ 3}{---}$]ων containing a reference to some division of the late Roman imperial army. We prefer the reading Ἐρούλων because this inscription agrees in several peculiar details with a number of documents in which members of the Herulian Corps are mentioned (see below).

In connection with μετα|κεινῆσαι in lines 6-7, see No. XIX and *I.G.*, II², 13209, 13210; Compare *S.E.G.*, VIII, no. 13. Kirchner correctly read the final letters of line 6. The phrase ἕτερόν τινα καταθέσθαι has been rightly restored by Robert (*Rev. de Phil.*, XVIII, 1944, p. 39, note 6) in *I.G.*, II², 13218.

In line 10, the reading ἱερῷ ταμείῳ is correct and complete, since this translation of the Latin *fiscus* occurs on several Greek Christian epitaphs from Concordia (*I.G.*, XIV, 2324, 2326, 2327, 2329, 2332, 2333). These tombstones from Concordia share with our inscription another peculiarity, for they too state the fine in pounds of metal (λεῖτραι).[173] Together with

---

[172] For three Christian epitaphs of soldiers belonging to *numeri*, see P. Perdrizet, *Mel. d'arch. et d'hist.*, XXV, 1905, pp. 85-86, no. 6 (from Salonica); W. K. Prentice, *Greek and Latin Inscriptions* (1908), p. 149, no. 141 (from Syria); D. M. Robinson, *T.A.P.A.*, LVII, 1926, pp. 215-216, no. 36 (from Asia Minor).

[173] See also L. Robert, *Rev. de Phil.*, XVIII, 1944, p. 37, note 9 (also on p. 38).

these Greek tombstones there were found a number of Latin epitaphs of Roman soldiers, two of whom belonged to the Herulian Corps (Dessau, nos. 2796 and 2801). To complete the link between these inscriptions from Concordia [174] and the Attic epitaph of Maiorinos, it should be noticed that the two Herulians (as well as some of the other mercenaries mentioned in Dessau, nos. 2796-2803) had the Roman *nomen* Flavius in addition to their native *cognomen*. At least one of these Roman soldiers was a Christian (Dessau, no. 2803), and it seems likely that they all belong to the same period as the Syrian Christians whose sarcophagi were found in the same cemetery (*I.G.*, XIV, 2324-2336). Three of these Greek epitaphs (*I.G.*, XIV, 2332, 2330, and 2333) are dated in the years 409/10, 418/9, 426/7, and all of them, Latin and Greek, should be dated in the beginning of the fifth century. It is tempting to assume that the tombstone of Maiorinos belongs to the same period. The inscription itself does not reveal whether or not Maiorinos was a Christian. No cross adorned his tombstone which is now almost completely preserved; see above, p. 13.

XXI (Plate IV). The inscription published by Konstantopoulos, *Harmonia*, no. 19, is now in the Epigraphical Museum (E.M. 9970). It is republished below because it shows several characteristics of the Attic Christian epitaphs.

†   [†]

Κοιμη[τήριον]

Ἰωά[ννου καὶ]

Μελ[ιτίας].

ϛ′   [ϛ′]

The large incised cross above the beginning of the inscription was probably balanced by another to the right; see above, note 76. There may also have been a second leaf below the restored part of the text; see above, note 98.

The three lines of the inscription are cut between four thin guide lines, which are *ca.* 0.022 m. apart; see above, note 138. The wide spacing of the first three letters of the name Ἰωά[ννου] makes it uncertain whether we should restore καί or κέ or the abbreviated form of this conjunction at the end of the line; see above, pp. 11-12.

The name in line 3 was tentatively restored by Konstantopoulos as Μελ[αίνης]. This name is not attested, and the genitive of the known form Μελαινίς would be too long. The restoration suggested above fills the available space.[175] The names Meletios and Melitios were well known during the fourth and fifth centuries after Christ (*R.E.*, *s. vv.*), and the corresponding feminine form would be Melitia. It has been suggested that this name be restored on another Christian inscription from Athens; see above, note 33.

XXII (Plate V). The inscription published by Konstantopoulos, *Harmonia,* no. 10, is now in the Epigraphical Museum (E.M. 9972). It is republished below because of the peculiar abbreviation of the word κοιμήτηριον.

✝   Κοιμητήρ(ιον)

Ἀνδρέου

καὶ Τύχης.

The stone is, according to Konstantopoulos, broken at the left, but it is clear that the text is completely preserved. The stonecutter abbreviated κοιμητήριον by putting a mark over the final rho; see above, p. 12.

For a discussion of the *crux monogrammatica* with the open rho, see above, p. 16. Attention should be called to the square sigma (see above, note 70); the epsilon, however, is of the lunate shape.

XXIII (Plate V). The inscription published by Konstantopoulos, *Harmonia,* no. 15, is now kept in the Epigraphical Museum (E.M. 9976).

---

[174] See C. Hülsen, *R.E.*, *s. v.* Concordia 1.

[175] Bechtel (*Personennamen*, p. 554), accents this name Μελίτεια, probably with reference to the city Μελίταια (*R.E.*, *s. v.*).

['Ο πα]μφιλέ[σ]
[τ]ạ[τ]ος
Διογένης
ἐνθάδε κῖτε
5 σὺν ὁμόφ⟨ρ⟩ο
νι γυνεκὶ
Σαμβατίδι.

Konstantopoulos' restoration of the first two lines ([οὗτος ?] ἄφιλος [λ]ίθος) is by no means as certain as he claims, and the meaning of this ἐπιφώνησις remains puzzling and unparalleled. Unless the stone is now more damaged than when Konstantopoulos examined it, his reading of [λ]ίθος in the second line must be rejected. The letter in front of ΦΙΛ in the first line may have been alpha, lambda, or mu, while the letter after ΦΙΛ was epsilon, theta, or omikron. No trace of the following sigma is now visible on the squeeze; see *Harmonia*, plate 3, no. 20.

In the second line, only OC can be read with certainty, and it seems that the letters in front were damaged (erased ?) even before the stone was broken.

The restoration [ὁ πα]μφιλέ[στ]ạ[τ]ος, although unique among the Attic epitaphs,[176] apparently corresponds to the expression ὁ (or ἡ) τὴν μακαρίαν μνήμην, which is often combined with ἐνθάδε κεῖται (see No. XIII). In line 5, the stonecutter wrote an iota for a rho. It is uncertain whether this is a mistake or an indication of a peculiar pronunciation.[177] For a discussion of the name Σαμβατίς, see below, No. 13.

The inscription is engraved between six thin guide lines, of which the first five are *ca.* 0.028 m. apart; see above, note 138. The last guide line slants markedly upward, and the last line of the inscription is engraved without regard to this line.

XII. THE NEW TEXTS

1 (Plate V). Inscribed pillar of Hymettian marble, found on February 10, 1936, in Section P. The right and left (?) edges, and the back, are preserved.

Height, 0.235 m.; width, 0.16 m.; thickness, 0.085 m.

Height of letters, 0.017-0.038 m.

Inv. No. I 3395.

Θεοδ
ωρήτ
ου
ἐνθάδε
5 [κ]ῖτε υἱ
[ὸς(?) ---].

The only indication that this inscription is Christian is provided by the name Theodoretos which is well attested for early Christian times but occurs otherwise in Attica only once, in a list of epheboi (*I.G.*, II², 2239, line 322).[178]

The text of the inscription as printed above might indicate that this was the tomb of Theodoretos' son whose name would have to be restored in the sixth line. It seems unlikely, however, that the name of the father would have been so prominently displayed, at the beginning of the inscription and in larger letters. It may be suggested, therefore, that the stone carried two inscriptions. The first recorded the death of Theodoretos, giving his name in the

[176] The adjective is found on a papyrus of the fifth or sixth century (Preisigke, *Wörterbuch*, III, p. 198); παμφιλεστάτῳ ἀδελφῷ Πέτρῳ.

[177] See E. Schwyzer, *Griechische Grammatik*, I, p. 212, notes 4 and 5.

[178] It may be noted that other Christian-sounding names are found in the ephebic catalogues of the third century after Christ, and the question may be raised whether or not some of the Attic epheboi may have been Christians. This problem is complicated by the fact that the majority of the early Christian names from Athens are known also as pagan names.

simple genitive. The second, beginning in line 4, although there was space in line 3, may have been the epitaph of Theodoretos' son: ἐνθάδε [κ]ῖτε υἱ[ὸς αὐτοῦ ———]. Good parallels are the inscriptions published in *C.G.–C.I.*, I, 1, nos. 34 and 60.

No definite date can be suggested for this epitaph, or for any of the other early Christian inscriptions published here. Attention may be called, however, to the horizontal strokes of the epsilon and of the theta which do not touch the curved part of the letters. This may be an indication of an early date, possibly in the fourth century.

2 (Plate V). Inscribed pillar of Hymettian marble, found on October 1, 1937, in Section AA. The stone is broken at the top, bottom, and back.

Height, 0.22 m.; width, 0.15 m.; thickness, 0.086 m.

Height of letters, *ca.* 0.018 m.

Inv. No. I 5017.

> ['Ενθάδε κῖ]
> τ[ε *ca. 4*]
> [ἡ] τοῦ ὑπ[ο]
> διακόνου
> 5 'Ονησιφόρου
> θυγάτηρ.

['Ενθάδε κῖ]τ[ε] is restored at the beginning because of the nominative in line 6. The office of ὑποδιάκονος occurs here for the first time in the Attic inscriptions; see above, note 45. It may be presumed that the daughter of the subdeacon died as a child, and that she was buried by her father. The name Onesiphoros is known from pagan inscriptions of the Roman period.

There is nothing peculiar about the letter forms except for the "Latin" delta at the beginning of the fourth line.[179]

3 (Plate V). Inscribed plaque of Pentelic marble, found on April 21, 1934, in Section K. Only the left side is preserved. Traces of a vertical incised line, running down from the upright stroke of the kappa, are visible.

Height, 0.11 m.; width, 0.095 m.; thickness, 0.045 m.

Height of letters, 0.008–0.012 m.

Inv. No. I 1837.

> Κοιμη
> τήριον
> 'Ανδρέα.

The fragment is broken on the right side, but the first three lines of the inscription are completely preserved. It may be that a fragment of a larger block was used for the Christian inscription, and the material, Pentelic marble, supports this assumption; see also No. 4. The fine lettering of the text indicates, however, considerable care in the preparation of this epitaph. It may be that the same stone contained two funerary inscriptions of which only the one on the left is preserved (see above, p. 7). For a discussion of the name Andreas, see No. XI.

Attention may be called to the occurrence of a square epsilon in line 3, but this form of the letter need not necessarily be taken as an indication of an early date, since it is also found combined with otherwise late letter forms; see above, note 70.

4 (Plate V). Inscribed plaque of Pentelic marble, found on April 16, 1937, in Section II. The back is smooth.

---

[179] Similar forms are found in two Christian epitaphs from Athens (Nos. XIII and 15), in a Jewish inscription from Athens (*I.G.*, III, 3546; see W. Larfeld, *Handbuch*, II, 2, pp. 502 and 506), and in two inscriptions from Corinth (*C.G.–C.I.*, I, 1, nos. 21 and 30, line 11 = *A.J.A.*, XXXV, 1931, p. 440, fig. 14). This form of delta, incidentally, is found in the Gothic alphabet as it originated toward the end of the fourth century after Christ; see A. Sigalas, 'Ιστορία τῆς 'Ελληνικῆς Γραφῆς, p. 290.

Height, 0.105 m.; width, 0.12 m.; thickness, 0.03 m.

Height of letters, 0.023 m.

Inv. No. I 4735.

[† Κοι]μη[τήριον]
['Ανδ]ρέου π[ρεσ]
[βυτέ]ρου κ[αὶ _ca. 3_ –]
[– – – – – – – –]

Instead of the epsilon in the second line, the stonecutter originally engraved a circular letter, probably in anticipation of the following omikron.

The preserved thickness of the fragment (0.03 m.) indicates that it belongs to a small plaque, and the letter forms, especially the open rho, suggest a date in the late Roman or early Christian period. The cross has been restored in front of [κοι]μη[τήριον] so that the second line may begin with the name ['Ανδ]ρέου. The third line was evidently spaced more narrowly than lines 1-2, and the restoration suggested above takes this fact into account.

For the occurrence of the name 'Ανδρέας (and of the genitive form in -ου), see above, pp. 20-21. For the restoration π[ρεσβυτέ]ρου see *I.G.*, III, 3449 = Bayet, no. 67.

5 (Plate VI). Inscribed plaque of Pentelic marble, found on April 19, 1936, in Section N. The stone is broken at the bottom and at the upper left corner.

Height, 0.145 m.; width, 0.245 m.; thickness, 0.05 m.

Height of letters, 0.02-0.03 m.

Inv. No. I 4088.

[Κ]υμητήρι
[ο]ν 'Ανδρέου

ἀναγνώ(στου)
τ(ῆς) 'Αγίας
5 'Αγαθο
κλίας.

The significance of this inscription lies in the fact that it mentions by name one of the oldest churches of Athens, dedicated to Saint Agathokleia. A church called 'Αγία 'Αγαθόκλεια is known to have existed in Athens, and its location on the ὁδὸς 'Ερμοῦ is near enough to the Agora to allow the assumption that it stood on the same site as its predecessor.[180] K. S. Pittakes, whose house stood near the church of St. Agathokleia, reports ('Εφ. 'Αρχ., 1856, no. 2686) that he and his neighbors saved the Ikon of the church at the time when Athens was set afire by the Turks during the Revolutionary War. The Ikon was taken to Salamis (an old refuge of the Athenians) and finally, after the liberation of Athens, deposited in the Μεγάλον Μοναστῆρι since the church of St. Agathokleia was completely destroyed.[181] The feast day of the Saint is still celebrated on the 17th of September in the Μεγάλον Μοναστῆρι which lies only a few yards from the old church. Pittakes suggested that the church of St. Agathokleia stood on the place of the pagan sanctuary of Eukleia and Eunomia, since many ancient inscriptions were found there.[182] Whatever may be the verdict on this hypothesis, it is now evident that the Church of St. Agathokleia dates back at least to the sixth or fifth century after Christ.

A. Mommsen has already collected (see note 182) some evidence concerning 'Αγία 'Αγαθόκλεια. From this it appears that her feast day fell on the 17th of September, and that she was a martyr. More can be learned from the

---

[180] See W. Judeich, *Topographie*², map I, E3, on ὁδὸς 'Ερμοῦ between ὁδὸς Πιττάκη and ὁδὸς 'Αγίας (the name of the church is given as ΑΓΙΑ ΟΙΚΟΝΟΜΟΙ); see above, p. 33.

[181] See A. Xyngopoulos, Εὑρετήριον, II, p. 114, no. 27; see also D. G. Kampouroglou, 'Αττικοὶ Ἔρωτες, pp. 48 and 57 (reporting that Byron lived during his first visit to Athens on ὁδὸς 'Αγίας, in the home of the Makri family).

[182] See K. S. Pittakys, *L'ancienne Athènes*, pp. 497 and 500; A. Mommsen, *Athenae Christianae*, p. 104, no. 123; *R.E.*, *s.v.* Eukleia; W. Judeich, *Topographie*², p. 399; *I.G.*, I², 77; *I.G.*, II², 4878 and the note on 5059; see also No. XIX of this publication.

famous *Menologium* of Basil II where, on the occasion of St. Agathokleia's feast day, the story of her martyrdom is told.[183] Agathokleia was a Christian slave girl belonging to Nikolaos and Paulina who were originally also Christians; in one source it is stated that only Nikolaos was a Christian while Paulina was a pagan. When Agathokleia's masters renounced their former Christian faith and again began to worship τὰ εἴδωλα, she refused to do the same. For several years she suffered insults and injuries, and was finally subjected to the most cruel punishment at the hands of Paulina. Agathokleia died as a blood witness. Although the church records do not seem to provide any information regarding the date and the place of Agathokleia's martyrdom, it may now be assumed, from the account of the *Menologium*, that it took place under Diocletian or even earlier, and the inscription published here may indicate that the story had its setting in Athens. There is, in fact, another early Christian epitaph from Athens on which the church of St. Agathokleia is mentioned: *I.G.*, III, 3480. The text of this inscription, of which no squeeze is available at Princeton, was first read and restored by Koumanoudes, *op. cit.*, no. 3582, and his restoration is now proved to be correct.[184]

It has been mentioned above that the Christian epitaphs found in the Agora belong to a cemetery located in or near the Agora. In addition to the church of St. George (the Hephaisteion), and the so-called Μεγάλη Παναγία (in the library of Hadrian), the church of St. Agathokleia may well be considered as one of the earliest, if not the earliest, church in the area of the Agora.

The letter forms of the inscription are different from those of the other inscriptions in two respects. The square forms of the letters sigma, omega, and especially of epsilon (see

above, note 70) seem to indicate an early date, while the opposite impression is gained from the use of abbreviations (see above, p. 11 and note 69) and from the occurrence of the ligature of omikron upsilon (see above, note 66). For a discussion of the office of ἀναγνώστης, see above, p. 8.

6 (Plate V). Inscribed pillar of Hymettian marble, found on December 31, 1936, in Section Y. The stone is broken at the upper left corner.

Height, 0.219 m.; width, 0.145 m.; thickness, 0.138 m.

Height of letters, *ca.* 0.02 m.

Inv. No. I 4290.

     [Οἱ] † κη
     [τ]ήριον
     Διονυσο
     δώρου [κὲ]
 5 Εὐτροπία[ς].

In line 4 [κέ] rather than [καί] is restored, for there does not seem to be enough space for the longer form.

It is interesting to notice that of the four letters of the first line two are engraved on each side of the incised cross; for this arrangement, see above, p. 15.

7 (Plate V). Inscribed plaque of Hymettian marble, found on March 26, 1937, in Section P. Only the inscribed face and the back are preserved.

Height, 0.11 m.; width, 0.09 m.; thickness, 0.025 m.

Height of letters, 0.019 m.-0.024 m.

Inv. No. I 4649.

   † Κυμη[τήριον]
   Ἐλπιδ[ίου (?)].

The restoration of the name is uncertain;

---

[183] J. P. Migne, *Patrologia Graeca*, CXVII, col. 53; the parallel evidence is assembled by A. Lambert, *Dict. d'hist. et de géogr. eccl.*, I, pp. 913-914. For the date of the *Menologium*, see S. Der Nersessian, *Byzantion*, XV, 1940-1941, pp. 104-125.

[184] The name Agathokleia occurs on two Christian epitaphs; one from Athens (*I.G.*, II², 13240 [see above, p. 7]) and one from Corinth (*C.G.-C.I.*, 1, no. 43); see also above, note 11.

Ἐλπιδ[ηφόρου] would fill the entire available space.

8 (Plate VI). Columnar grave monument of Hymettian marble, found on June 7, 1935, in Section Ν′. The original top and almost the full diameter are preserved; the surface is badly worn.

Height, 0.60 m.; original diameter, about 0.18 m.

Height of letters, *a*: 0.022 m.; *b*: 0.017-0.025 m.

Inv. No. I 2979.

a   [ca. 2]ίνων   *ca.* 100 B.C
    ['Ηρακ]λεώτης.
b   † Κυμ[ητήριον]
    Εὐκα[ρπίο]υ
    καὶ 'Αγά[πης]. †

Of the Christian inscription only the beginning and the end are preserved. It is assumed that the cross appearing on the left side of the illustration marks the end of the inscription, and that the trace of a letter above it belongs to the second line of the text. The restoration of the names in both inscriptions is uncertain.

This is one of the many Christian epitaphs which are engraved on small columns, the so-called *columellae* or κιονίσκοι; see above, note 143. For a discussion of reused stones, see above, p. 23.

9 (Plate VI). Inscribed plaque of Hymettian marble, found on March 16, 1937, in Section Σ. Parts of all faces are preserved; all faces are very crudely dressed except the inscribed face. The space below the inscription, 0.15 m. high, was left unworked for insertion in the ground.

Height, 0.425 m.; width, 0.281 m.; thickness, 0.101 m.

Height of letters, 0.020-0.028 m.

Inv. No. I 4637.

        ϭ′ † ƍ
    Κυμητήρι
    ον ['Ιω]άνη
    [κ]αὶ Εὐκαρπίας.

The name in the second line cannot be restored with certainty. There is a rather wide uninscribed space before the alpha. Traces of the omega may be visible in the break. The narrow space between this omega and the final nu of κυμητήριον could have been filled only by an iota. It is tempting to restore ['Ιω]άνη, and to assume that it was written with only one nu (see above, note 126); for this form of the genitive, see above, p. 21.

The design above the inscription, a cross flanked by two leaves, is common among the Attic tombstones, while it does not seem to occur elsewhere; see above, p. 15.

10 (Plate VI). Inscribed plaque of Pentelic marble, found on February 10, 1939, in Section MM. The top, beveled right side, and back of the stone are preserved. The back is smooth, and shows signs of having been cut by a saw; the fragment seems to be part of an old revetment reused as a tombstone; see above, note 145.

Height, 0.16 m.; width, 0.115 m.; thickness, 0.025-0.032 m.

Height of letters, *ca.* 0.025 m.

Inv. No. I 5676.

    [Κοιμ]ητή
    [ριον] Εὐφρο
    [σύνο]υ.

The wide space between the second and third lines may indicate that the inscription contained only one name.

11 (Plate VI). Inscribed plaque of Hymettian marble, found on December 15, 1937, in Section Ω. The right side is preserved.

Height, 0.225 m.; width, 0.15 m.; thickness, 0.051 m.

Height of letters, *ca.* 0.023 m.

Inv. No. I 5089.

    [Κοι]μη
    [τίρι] † ον
    [διαφέ]ρον
    [Λέον]τος
5   [κὲ Θεοδ]ούλης.

The reading of the first line is very uncertain, but the position of the letters of the second line after the horizontal bars of the cross makes it likely that the inscription was carved above and on both sides of the cross. Thus, considering the faint traces above the second line, one may also restore [οἰ]κη[τίρι]ον. The word διαφέρον (often written διαφέροντα) is usually followed by the proper name in the dative, but in several instances is construed with the genitive.[185]

For the cross which intersects the first four lines, see above, p. 15. There hardly seems to be space even for the short form κέ at the beginning of the fifth line, and it may be that an abbreviation for καί was used (see above, pp. 11-12). What seems to be the trace of a letter (upsilon ?), which is visible below the upsilon of the fifth line, may be either a mark of damage on the stone or part of an incised cross (or other ornament) below the inscription. If it should, however, be part of the text, an alternative restoration may be suggested for the fifth and sixth lines: [κὲ τῆς δ]ούλης [αὐτο]ῦ; compare N. I. Giannopoulos, *Byz. Zeitschr.*, XXI, 1912, pp. 152-153, no. 1 = G. A. Soteriou, Ἀρχ. Ἐφ., 1929, p. 155, no. 12.

12 (Plate VII). Columnar grave monument of Hymettian marble, found in January, 1937, in Section Σ. The top and about one fourth of the circumference are preserved.

Height, 0.236 m.; width, 0.14 m.; thickness, 0.129 m.

Height of letters, *ca.* 0.02 m.

Inv. No. I 4452.

a [---]ας   *ca.* 100 B.C.
   [---]ωνος
   [---]ιος.

b † Ọ[---]
   κὲ Ḥ[---]

The Christian inscription (*b*) probably consists of two names in the genitive case connected by καί, spelled here κέ. For the shape of the gravestone, and for its earlier use as a pagan tombstone, see above, notes 143 and 144.

13 (Plate VII). Columnar grave monument of Hymettian marble, found on March 16, 1936, in Section Σ. The stone is broken above and below, but the circumference is preserved.

Height, 0.165 m.; diameter, 0.106 m.

Height of letters, 0.022-0.032 m.

Inv. No. I 3813.

[† Κο]ιμ[ητήριο]ν
Σαμβατίδος. †

For the use of columns as Christian tombstones, see above, p. 23.

The name Σαμβατίς occurs only once in pre-Christian Athens (*I.G.*, II², 7931: tombstone of a woman from Ankara), but this and similar names are surprisingly frequent among the Christian Athenians.[186] Bayet suggested (p. 36) that these names are derived from the name of the Holy Sabbath, but it may be that the name of Emperor Justinian's father (Sabbatios, Σαββάτης) also was not without effect on their popularity.[187]

14 (Plate VIII). Inscribed plaque of Pentelic marble, found on November 8, 1935, in Section N. The inscribed face, the roughly picked top, the left side, and the back are preserved. Traces of a vertical line, continuing the upright stroke of the kappa, are visible.

Height, 0.225 m.; width, 0.13 m.; thickness, 0.073 m.

[185] See No. 24; I. Ch. Dragarses, Παρνασσός, VI, 1882, p. 252; *I.G.*, IV, 403; G. A. Soteriou, Ἀρχ. Ἐφ., 1929, p. 150 (no. 2), 153 (no. 9), 155 (no. 13), 157 (no. 22); *Corinth*, VIII, 1, no. 148; *C.G.–C.I.*, I, 1, nos. 3, 17, 31-34, 37, 39.

[186] In addition to *I.G.*, III, 3460, 3525; No. XXIII, and G. A. Soteriou, Εὑρετήριον, I, p. 10, fig. 2, mention may be made of three unpublished inscriptions in the Epigraphical Museum (E.M. 2225, 3425 + 4753, 5672); compare also *C.I.G.*, IV, 9723 and *I.G.*, XII, 1, no. 693.

[187] See Nagl, *R.E.*, *s. v.* Sabbatius: compare also D. M. Robinson, *T.A.P.A.*, LVII, 1926, p. 216; Bees, *op. cit.*, p. 75, note 2.

Height of letters, 0.014-0.025 m.

Inv. No. I 3200.

Κυμ[ητήριον]
Σχολ[αστικ]
οῦ.

Scholastikos as a proper name occurs in the fifth century after Christ, and this inscription may be one of its earliest occurrences.

15 (Plate VII). Inscribed plaque of Pentelic marble, found on March 22, 1934, in Section K. The upper left corner is broken away.

Height, 0.66 m.; width, 0.275 m.; thickness, 0.05 m.

Height of letters, 0.015-0.035 m.

Inv. No. I 1657.

[Κοιμη]τύριον
[___ca.4___ ὅσ]τις ἂν
[ἐπι]τη
δεύσῃ δη(νάρια) πέν
5 τε χρούσινα
κὲ τὴν ἀρχον
τικὴν τιμου
ρίαν ὑποστῆν(αι).

The name to be restored in the second line must have been very short, but this is the only place where a proper name can be supplied. The phrase [ὅσ]τις ἂν [ἐπι]τηδεύσῃ is unusual, but it exactly corresponds to the common formula εἰ δέ τις τολμήσει found in many pagan and Christian documents.[188] The verb ἐπιτηδεύω (in the meaning " to do with deliberate purpose ") may be here confused with ἐπικηδεύω which has (according to Hesychios, s. v. ψέγω) the meaning " to make an additional burial." [189] It is significant that threats introduced by the phrase

εἰ δέ τις ἐπιτηδεύσει (or similar phrases containing the verb ἐπιτηδεύω) occur very frequently on Christian tombstones from Phrygia and occasionally on inscriptions from Cilicia.[190] The Attic inscription published here may well have been composed by somebody familiar with the phraseology used in Phrygia, but the rest of the text (lines 5-8) shows no similarity to examples from Asia Minor. The letters ΔΗ, in line 4, may be an abbreviation for δη(νάρια); see M. Avi-Yonah, *Abbreviations in Greek Inscriptions*, p. 58. They may also represent the verb δεῖ, in which case ὑποστῆν(αι) would depend on it. Instead of the tau, in line 6, the stonecutter originally engraved the horizontal stroke of an eta, the letter which follows in the text. The last word of the inscription, ὑποστῆν(αι), if ΔΗ stands for δη(νάρια), is an infinitive, here practically equivalent to an imperative. It is used here in the meaning " to undertake unwillingly, to submit to, to endure," and it is probably a synonym of ὑπόκειμαι which occurs frequently in similar texts. The ending may have been omitted by mistake, or the engraver (or the composer) of the text may have thought that -ην = ειν was the infinitive ending.

The main part of the inscription (lines 2-8) is taken up by a threat against a possible violator of the tomb (or the tombstone).[191] The interesting feature of this inscription lies in the mention of a fine imposed upon the violator, and in the currency of this fine. The Attic pagan inscriptions in which fines are mentioned (*I.G.*, II², 13211, 13215, 13219 [see above, No. XX]) use silver as currency except for *I.G.*, II², 13224 (χρυσοῦ ὠκίας τρῖς) and 13220 which imposes the fine of 25 *denarii* without stating the kind of metal.[192] Considering the value of

---

[188] For the occurrence of ἄν, see *I.G.*, II², 13214; J. Keil and A. Wilhelm, *M.A.M.A.*, III, p. 73 (no. 77); W. M. Ramsay, *Cities and Bishoprics of Phrygia*, II, pp. 514 (no. 353) and 529 (no. 373).

[189] See also *S.E.G.*, VI, no. 784, and Ramsay, *op. cit.*, II, pp. 535 (no. 391) and 542 (no. 408).

[190] See Ramsay, *op. cit., passim*; W. H. Buckler and W. M. Calder, *M.A.M.A.*, VI, pp. 72-88; J. Keil and A. Wilhelm, *op. cit.*, III, pp. 73 (no. 77) and 174 (no. 504); *S.E.G.*, VI, 268 and 784; compare B. Keil, *Hermes*, XLIII, 1908, p. 533.

[191] For a discussion of this type of inscription, see above, pp. 9-11.

[192] The inscriptions published as *I.G.*, II², 13212, 13217, 13218, 13221 are not Attic; see above, note 49.

the silver *denarius* in that period (third century after Christ), it may be assumed that the 25 *denarii* mentioned in *I.G.*, II², 13220 were in fact gold *denarii*. The usage of *denarii aurei* is well attested for the later Roman empire,[193] and the Greek equivalent (χρύσινοι) is well attested for central Greece.[194] The same term is used in another Attic text (G. Lampakes, Δελτίον τῆς Χριστ. Ἀρχ. Ἑτ., I, 1892, p. 67; see also Bees, *op. cit.*, p. 88) the last two lines of which read: ἴ τις δὲ ἐπιχιρήση, χρύσινα δ[– – –]. The final letter delta may stand for the numeral ten, or it may be the beginning of the word δ[ηνάρια], possibly abbreviated.

The amount of the fine of five gold pieces is well above the normal price of a tomb, which was about one and a half solidi; see De Waele in Bees, *op. cit.*, p. 57.

The second part of the threat, τὴν ἀρχοντικὴν τιμουρίαν [195] probably refers to corporal punishment. For the office of the "Archon" who is to exact the punishment, see E. Hanton, *Byzantion*, IV, 1927-1928, pp. 67-68. In pagan times, the fine was paid to the treasurer of the Areopagus.

The tombstone is one of the largest of its kind, comparable in size, though not in workmanship, to *I.G.*, III, 3486 (height, 0.56 m.; width, 0.26 m.) and 3509 (height, 0.50 m.; width, 0.24 m.). The large incised cross, around which the first six lines of the inscription are engraved, finds its parallel in the somewhat larger cross on *I.G.*, III, 3463, where the inscription is arranged in a similar manner; see above, p. 15. For other examples of the "Latin" delta which occurs twice in line 4, see above, note 179.

A fragment of another similar document written around a cross was published in *Harmonia*, no. 12; it is now in the Epigraphical Museum (E.M. 9973). According to Konstantopoulos, one face of this plaque (which is 0.03 m. thick) contained an almost entirely preserved incised cross within which the words Ἡ μακαρία Παῦλα were inscribed. The other face (which is illustrated here on Plate VIII) contained a large incised cross, of which only the right cross bar remains. Less than half of the width is therefore preserved, and there may have been another cross (with the name of Paula's husband inscribed within ?) on the obverse side of the plaque.

```
        ΛΣШΦ
        ΣΟΥΑ
        ΗΔΕ
    †   ΤΑΝ
[Α]     Ш ΥΠΟ
        ΙΣΤΟΝΕΝ
        ΣΕΜ
```

The four horizontal guide lines which appear on this inscription are *ca.* 0.025 m. apart. The vertical guide line at the right of the cross was drawn to facilitate the engraving of the incised cross; see above, p. 22. Like Konstantopoulos, we too are unable to suggest a restoration. The last letter in the first line may be a phi and not a sigma (as Konstantopoulos suggests), for the sigmas in lines 2 and 6 are square; see above, note 70. Konstantopoulos (both in his text and on plate 3, 13) failed to report the final nu in line 4. The large omega which stands under the right arm of the cross

---

[193] See Hultsch, *R.E.*, *s.v.* denarius, col. 214, no. 15; H. Ingholt, *Berytus*, III, 1936, pp. 110-111; A. Segrè, *Byzantion*, XV, 1940-1941, pp. 272-275; L. C. West and A. C. Johnson, *Currency in Roman and Byzantine Egypt*, pp. 137-139.

[194] See *I.G.*, IV, 190 (Aigina; see E. L. Sukenik, *Ancient Synagogues in Palestine and Greece*, p. 44, plate 11), 437 (Sikyon); VII, 26 (Megara, *ca.* 470 A.D.); *C.G.–C.I.*, I, 1, nos. 30-32 (Corinth). For the spelling χρούσινα = χρύσινα, see above, note 119.

[195] Like τῇ κεφαλητικῇ τιμωρίᾳ; see Preisigke, *Wörterbuch*, II, *s.v.* τιμωρία, and, especially, *S.E.G.*, VII, no. 171: κεφαλικὴν ὑπομένι τιμωρίαν; compare also *S.E.G.*, VIII, No. 13. For the spelling of τιμουρία = τιμωρία, see above, note 120.

must have been balanced by a corresponding alpha under the left arm of the cross (see above, note 91), and does not, therefore, belong to the text of the inscription. There are traces of a seventh line. Only the epsilon is clearly visible. It may have been preceded by tau or sigma, and followed by mu or omega.

16 (Plate VIII). Inscribed plaque of coarse marble with greenish veins, found in 1931, in Section B. The stone is broken on all sides.

Height, 0.14 m.; width, 0.105 m.; thickness, 0.047 m.

Height of letters, *ca.* 0.035 m.

Inv. No. I 152.

$$[\text{Κατοι}] \quad \dagger \quad κη[τή]$$
$$[ριον] \quad Πω[- \, ^{2-3} \, -]$$
$$[- - - - - - - -]$$

It is assumed that the large incised cross stood in the middle of the first line; for this type of arrangement, see above, p. 15. For the use of [κατοι]κη[τήριον], see *I.G.*, III, 3508; compare No. XIII (κατοικῖ). Another possible restoration of the first line would be [θή] † κη.[196] The main objection to this restoration is the large size of the letters, *ca.* 0.035 m., and the thickness of the stone (0.047 m.), both of which indicate that the plaque was of considerable width. The letters of the second line (Πω) belong to the name of the deceased.

17 (Plate VIII). Inscribed plaque of Pentelic marble, found on May 12, 1933, in Section Z. Part of the right side and the smooth back are preserved.

Height, 0.096 m.; width, 0.12 m.; thickness, 0.06 m.

Height of letters, *ca.* 0.022 m.

Inv. No. I 789.

$$[\text{Κοιμητήρ}]ιον$$
$$[\underline{ca.\,6}]ξας$$
$$[κὲ \, \underline{ca.\,5} \, o]ν.$$

The restoration of this fragment as a Christian tombstone is uncertain. It is assumed that the name of the husband follows that of his wife; this order is exceptional; see above, note 32.

18 (Plate VIII). Inscribed plaque of Hymettian marble, found on May 10, 1933, in Section Θ. The upper left corner may be preserved.

Height, 0.176 m.; width, 0.105 m.; thickness, 0.033 m.

Height of letters, 0.039-0.053 m.

Inv. No. I 801.

$$\dagger \; \text{K}[υμιτ]$$
$$ιριο[ν \; 'A]$$
$$νδ[ρέα].$$

The restoration of the name is uncertain, and the division of κ[υμιτ]ίριον is unusual; see *I.G.*, III, 3450 (= Bayet, no. 125 and plate II, no. 6). For the spelling of κ[υμιτ]ίριον; see above, note 109.

19 (Plate VIII). Inscribed plaque of Pentelic marble, found on March 6, 1934, in Section K. The stone is broken above, below and at the left.

Height, 0.165 m.; width, 0.16 m.; thickness, 0.043 m.

Height of letters, 0.016-0.034 m.

Inv. No. I 1527.

$$\text{A} \quad \dagger \quad ω$$
$$[\text{Μνη}]μόριον$$
$$[\underline{ca.\,4}]τον \; κ[ὲ]$$
$$[- - -]$$

For a discussion of the symbols at the top of this epitaph, see above, notes 75 and 91. The word μνημόριον occurs on several other Attic funerary inscriptions: *I.G.*, III, 3493 ([μνη]-μήριον), 3513 (μνημόριον), 3530 ([μ]νημόριν); *I.G.*, II², 11782 (μνημόριν). Instead of κ[έ] at the end of the second line, there may have been used the abbreviation for καί; see above, pp. 11-12.

---

[196] This term occurs in Bayet, no. 84 (restored), Ἀρχ. Ἐφ., 1925-1926, p. 97, fig. 2, and, in a different position, in *I.G.*, III, 3509, line 4; it is also found among the pagan inscriptions (*I.G.*, II², 12525).

20 (Plate VIII). Inscribed plaque of Pentelic marble, found on March 16, 1936, in Section Σ. The back, with traces of a moulding at the top (from an earlier use), is preserved.

Height, 0.074 m.; width, 0.076 m.; thickness, 0.034 m.

Height of letters, 0.016-0.021 m.

Inv. No. I 3817.

$$[Κοι]μητ[ήριον]$$
$$[Φιλ]οπο[---]$$

It is assumed that the word $[κοι]μητ[ήριον]$ did not extend into the second line because the three preserved letters of this line, οπο, apparently belong to the middle of a name. The restoration of this name is uncertain; among possibilities are $[Καλ]οπο[---]$ and $[Θε]ο$-$πο[---]$.

21 (Plate IX). Inscribed plaque of Hymettian marble, found on March 29, 1919, in Section BB.

Height, 0.075 m.; width, 0.115 m.; thickness, 0.083 m.

Height of letters, ca. 0.025 m.

Inv. No. I 5744.

$$[Κυμη]τήριο[ν]$$
$$[Θεοφ]άντ[ου].$$

The restoration of the name is uncertain. A pair of guide lines (ca. 0.003 m. apart) appear below the letters of the first line, and another single guide line (ca. 0.012 m. below the second of these) appears above the letters of the second line; see above, note 138.

22 (Plate IX). Inscribed plaque of Island marble, found on March 20, 1936, in Section N. Part of the upper left corner is preserved.

Height, 0.115 m.; width, 0.064 m.; thickness, 0.052 m.

Height of letters, 0.025-0.035 m.

Inv. No. I 3797.

† $Κ[οιμητήριον]$
$τω[-^{ca.\ 9}-]$

The restoration depends on the reading of the second letter of line 2. The remains of a curved stroke near the top, and the trace of a horizontal base-stroke would clearly suggest an omega, but there is no certain occurrence of this early form of the letter in any other Christian text from Athens.[197] Assuming that an omega may be read, the restoration $τῶ[ν$ $μακαρίων]$ is suggested by *I.G.*, III, 3440. If the traces of the omega are disregarded, the first two lines may be restored as † $Κ[οιμη]$-$τ[ήριον]$.

23 (Plate IX). Inscribed plaque of Pentelic marble, found on April 24, 1936, in Section Σ. Part of the left side is preserved.

Height, 0.186 m.; width, 0.087 m.; thickness, 0.076 m.

Height of letters, ca. 0.014 m.

Inv. No. I 4062.

† $Κυ[μητήρι]$
$ον\ [-^{ca.\ 5}-]$
$εον\ [-^{ca.\ 4}-]$
$λο[---].$

The epitaph probably recorded the death of a man and his wife; their names cannot be restored with certainty. It seems likely that the husband's name stood first, and that it ended in line 3, where the final upsilon of the genitive ending omikron upsilon is partially preserved. It may have been followed by καί and a woman's name, or by a word indicating the man's occupation. There is an uninscribed space below, which indicates that this was the last line of the inscription.

24 (Plate IX). Inscribed plaque of Pentelic marble, found on June 7, 1933, in Section H. The stone is broken on all sides.

Height, 0.10 m.; width, 0.12 m.; thickness, 0.035 m.

[197] See, however, Bayet, no. 58 = *I.G.*, III, 3501; compare, for a late example of the early omega, S. N. Marinatos, Ἐπετηρίς, VII, 1930, p. 390, fig. 2.

Height of letters, 0.015-0.02 m.

Inv. No. I 948.

$$[-\overset{ca.\ 7}{-}]\lambda\acute{\iota}\rho[v]$$
$$[\delta\iota\alpha\phi\acute{\epsilon}\rho o]v\tau\alpha\ \Sigma\omega$$
$$[\dagger\ \overset{ca.\ 6}{-\ -}]\chi\alpha\varsigma.\ \dagger$$

The Christian character of the inscription is indicated by the trace of a cross after the sigma of the third line (only the upright of the cross is visible in the photograph). No convincing restoration is suggested for the text. The letters NTA, in line 2, may belong to the end of the word $[\delta\iota\alpha\phi\acute{\epsilon}\rho o]v\tau\alpha$,[198] but the lacuna in line 3 seems to be too long for restoring in it a woman's name: $\Sigma\omega[-\overset{ca.\ 6}{-}-]\chi\alpha$. For the construction of $\delta\iota\alpha\phi\acute{\epsilon}\rho o v$ with the genitive, see above, note 185. The letters of the first line may contain the end of a name.

25 (Plate IX). Inscribed plaque of Pentelic marble, found on February 1, 1934, in Section Z. Parts of the roughly picked top and of the smooth back are preserved; the other sides are broken.

Height, 0.095 m.; width, 0.152 m.; thickness, 0.06 m.

Height of letters, 0.022 m.

Inv. No. I 1247.

$$[\ \dagger\ ]\ \dagger\ \dagger$$
$$[\kappa o\iota\mu\eta]\tau\acute{\eta}\rho[\iota o v]$$

Above the first line, three tall and narrow crosses were engraved, the left one of which has to be restored; for a discussion of this arrangement, see above, p. 14.

26 (Plate IX). Inscribed plaque of Pentelic marble, found on March 5, 1936, in Section MM. The thin stone which originally served as a revetment is broken on top and bottom.

Height, 0.38 m.; width, 0.22 m.; thickness, 0.02 m.

Height of letters, 0.032 m.

Inv. No. I 3672.

$$[\mathrm{K}o\iota\mu\eta]$$
$$[\tau\acute{\eta}\rho\iota o v]$$
$$[-\overset{ca.\ 4}{-}]\acute{\iota}\alpha\varsigma$$
$$['\mathrm{A}\lambda]\epsilon\xi\alpha v$$
5 $$[\delta]\rho\acute{\iota}v\eta\varsigma.$$

It is assumed that this is a Christian tombstone because the name occurs in the genitive, depending presumably on $\kappa o\iota\mu\eta\tau\acute{\eta}\rho\iota o v$ which has been restored in the first two lines. The form of the ethnic (see above, note 38) $['\mathrm{A}\lambda]\epsilon\xi\alpha v$-$[\delta]\rho\acute{\iota}v\eta$ instead of the common Attic form $'\mathrm{A}\lambda\epsilon\xi\alpha v\delta\rho\hat{\iota}\tau\iota\varsigma$ (*I.G.*, II², 8002, 8007, 8009, 8010, 8013, 8019, 8024-8026, 8030, 8037, 8038) may be another indication of the Christian character although this form of the ethnic is attested by Strabo (XIII, 1, 36) and, for the Hadrianic period, by Stephanos (*s. v.* $'\mathrm{A}\lambda\epsilon\xi\acute{\alpha}v\delta\rho\epsilon\iota\alpha\iota$): $\mathrm{N}\iota$-$\kappa\acute{\alpha}v\omega\rho\ \delta\grave{\epsilon}\ \acute{o}\ '\mathrm{E}\rho\mu\epsilon\acute{\iota}o v\ \acute{\epsilon}v\ \tau\hat{\eta}\ \pi\epsilon\rho\grave{\iota}\ '\mathrm{A}\lambda\epsilon\xi\alpha v\delta\rho\epsilon\acute{\iota}\alpha\varsigma\ \pi\rho\acute{\omega}\tau\eta$ $\tau\alpha\hat{v}\tau\alpha\ \pi\acute{\alpha}v\tau\alpha\ \kappa v\rho o\hat{\iota},\ \kappa\alpha\grave{\iota}\ \tau\grave{o}\ '\mathrm{A}\lambda\epsilon\xi\alpha v\delta\rho\hat{\iota}v o\varsigma\ \kappa\alpha\grave{\iota}\ \tau\grave{o}$ $'\mathrm{A}\lambda\epsilon\xi\alpha v\delta\rho\acute{\iota}v\eta\varsigma$ (probably for $'\mathrm{A}\lambda\epsilon\xi\alpha v\delta\rho\acute{\iota}v\eta$), $o\grave{v}$ $\mu\acute{\epsilon}v\tau o\iota\ \tau\grave{o}\ '\mathrm{A}\lambda\epsilon\xi\alpha v\delta\rho\epsilon\acute{\omega}\tau\eta\varsigma$. Attention may also be called to the use of guide-lines (*ca.* 0.035 m. apart) which has been observed on many other early Christian inscriptions (see above, note 138), and to the fact that the plaque originally served as a revetment (see above, note 145).

27 (Plate IX). Inscribed plaque of Pentelic marble, found on May 25, 1936, in Section Σ. The back is smooth.

Height, 0.068 m.; width, 0.081 m.; thickness, 0.02 m.

Height of letters, *ca.* 0.025 m.

Inv. No. I 4207.

$$[\mathrm{K}o\iota\mu\eta\tau\acute{\eta}]\rho\iota o v$$

This stone originally served as a revetment, and was reused as a Christian tombstone; see above, note 145. There is a thin guide line above the letters, and another one *ca.* 0.028 m. below; see above, note 138. This fragment may belong to the same epitaph as No. 26. Their thickness is identical, and they both originally

---

[198] See *I.G.*, III, 3477, 3511; *C.G.–C.I.*, I, 1, nos. 33, 43, 59, 62; *Corinth*, VIII, 1, no. 148.

served as revetments. Yet the distance between the guide lines is not the same, and the letters on No. 26 seem to be smaller and more crowded.

28 (Plate IX). Inscribed pillar of Pentelic marble, found in the summer of 1933, in the southwest corner of Section Z. The stone is broken away at the bottom and along the left edge. On the right side is a moulding from an earlier use of the stone; see above, note 145. Part of a dowel cutting is visible on top, and a pivot hole for a door can be seen at the lower end of the inscribed face. The inscribed surface is crumbly, and little can be read except for the first two lines.

Height, 0.585 m.; width, 0.16 m.; thickness, 0.14 m.

Height of letters, *ca.* 0.023 m.

Inv. No. I 1061.

$$†$$
$$[\text{K}]υμη$$
$$[τ]ήριον$$
$$[- - -]$$
$$[- - -]$$
$$5 \quad [-^{ca.\,3}-]_{\iota\tau}$$

The letter read as tau in line 5 may be part of the inscription which continued beyond this line; or it may be a cross indicating the end of the text.

29 (Plate IX). Inscribed plaque of Pentelic marble, found on June 10, 1931, in Section E. The back and the curved right side are preserved.

Height, 0.295 m.; width, 0.13 m.; thickness, 0.03 m.

Height of letters, 0.022 m.

Inv. No. I 24.

$$[Κοιμητήρι]ον.$$
$$[\;☧\;]\;☧$$

The fragment apparently belongs to the upper part of a peculiarly shaped grave stele. There are traces of letters (or of an ornament ?) visible above the one line of the inscription. The restoration of this line is uncertain, in fact it is unlikely to be correct if the cross below stood exactly underneath the centre of the line; a second cross has therefore been restored. The cross is in the form of the *crux monogrammatica* with the closed rho; see above, p. 16.

30 (Plate X). Inscribed plaque of Pentelic marble, found on February 22, 1939, in Section MM. The left edge and back of the stone are preserved. The back is smooth, and shows signs of having been cut by a saw; the fragment was apparently used before as a revetment; see above, note 145.

Height, 0.125 m.; width, 0.082 m.; thickness, 0.015 m.

Height of letters, *ca.* 0.02 m.

Inv. No. I 5677.

$$μ[- - - -]$$
$$ει[- - -]$$
$$ιν[- - -]$$

There is an uninscribed space below the last line. The three guide lines are *ca.* 0.024 m. apart; see above, note 138. It is tempting to restore the last line as ἰν[δικτιῶνος] (probably abbreviated), for this word is found on one early Christian epitaph from Athens.[199]

31 (Plate X). Inscribed plaque of Hymettian marble, found on November 28, 1938, in Section EE. The stone is broken on all sides, but the back is preserved. A heavy line separates the first line of the text from the following lines.

Height, 0.125 m.; width, 0.168 m.; thickness, 0.042 m.

Height of letters, 0.02 m.

---

[199] *I.G.*, III, 3486. Mention of the indiction occurs frequently on the Christian epitaphs from Corinth; see *C.G.–C.I.*, I, 1, nos. 31, 34, 44, 49, 53 (= *Corinth*, VIII, 1, no. 164), 58 (= *Corinth*, VIII, 1, no. 170), 60, 62; *Corinth*, VIII, 1, nos. 147, 151, 162, 163, 167.

Inv. No. I 5631.

$$\text{'I}(\eta\sigma o\hat{v})\text{s X}[(\rho\iota\sigma\tau\acute{o})\text{s}]$$

† Μαιτᾶ[τον – – –]
τ̣ουτο [– – –]

For the occurrence of 'I(ησοῦ)s X[(ριστό)s] at the beginning of a funerary inscription, see Bayet, no. 10 (see above, note 7). This monogram may have continued with K(ύριο)s or with the verb Νικᾷ (possibly abbreviated; see above, note 59). The thickness of the stone (0.042 m.) shows that the original width cannot have been much more than twice the width of the preserved fragment. Thus about half of the second and third lines is preserved. The restoration μαιτᾶ[τον], or μαιτα[τώριον], suggested by H. Grégoire, assumes a peculiar spelling of this word. *Metatum* is used in medieval Latin in the meaning of *aedes propria, domicilium, interdum hospitium,* and was transcribed in Greek as μιτάτον.[200] It also occurs, however, in the spelling μητᾶτον, and is given the translation " mansion, lodging "; from it is derived μητατώριον, " the deacon's place in the inner sanctuary." [201] If the inscription under discussion is an epitaph, μητᾶτον may here be used in the same meaning as οἰκητήριον or οἶκος αἰώνιος. G. Soteriou suggested reading and restoring μαιτὰ (for μετὰ) τῶν ἁγίων.

32 (Plate X). Inscribed fragment of a block of Hymettian marble, found on January 3, 1935, in Section ΙΙ. The stone is broken at the left and at the bottom; both top and back are smoothly picked. The block was reused for the Christian inscription; see above, note 145.

Height, 0.235 m.; width, 0.147 m.; thickness, 0.495 m.

Height of letters, 0.03 m.

Inv. No. I 2280.

[– – –]ος †
[– – –]τον

The great thickness of the stone (0.495 m.) shows that this is no ordinary tombstone. The word to which the three letters of the second line belong (possibly a name) may have continued in a third line which did not extend over the full width of the stone.

33 (Plate X). Plaque of Hymettian marble, found in 1933, in Section H. The left side and part of the bottom and back are preserved.

Height, 0.155 m.; width, 0.15 m.; thickness, 0.055 m.

Height of letters, *ca.* 0.008 m.

Inv. No. I 1070.

$$\overline{\text{K}}(\acute{v}\rho\iota)\bar{\epsilon}\ \nu\acute{\iota}\kappa\alpha$$
$$[\sigma\omega]\tau\acute{\eta}\rho.$$

The line over the first two letters ($\overline{\text{KE}}$) indicates an abbreviation; see above, note 59. It is clear that the second letter is an epsilon and not a sigma. The vocative abbreviation of this name does occur on an inscription from Asia Minor (*M.A.M.A.*, I, no. 434), but the phrase Χριστὸς νικᾷ is found on many Christian inscriptions; see, for example, W. K. Prentice, *Greek and Latin Inscriptions* (1908), nos. 124, 201, and 219. The restoration of the second line is fairly certain, although only the letters tau and eta-rho (in ligature) are preserved. It is probable that we should read Κύριε σωτὴρ νίκα (Lord Saviour Conquer), or, if the nominative was really meant, Κύριος σωτὴρ νικᾷ.

The large Greek cross, cut within a raised circle, apparently covered most of the front face of the stone. If this was a tombstone, the name of the deceased was probably written in the lower right corner, or above the cross. The bird in the lower left corner was probably balanced by another at the right; see above, note 96. We illustrate here *Harmonia*, no. 22, now kept in the Epigraphical Museum (E.M. 9981), because it shows the same type of cross as the Agora inscription (see above, note 77),

---

[200] See Du Cange, *Glossarium, s. v. metare.*
[201] See Sophocles, *Greek Lexikon, s. v. μητᾶτον* and *s. v. μητατώριον*; compare *S.E.G.*, VII, no. 110.

and thus helps in the dating of the latter. Without this parallel, one may be inclined to date No. 33 in a later period, but it may well belong to the fifth or sixth century.

E.M. 9989 ω † A
Κοιμη[τήριο]
ν Ἐπα[γάθου].

For the omega alpha, see above, note 92; for the guide lines, which are *ca.* 0.025 m. apart, see above, note 138. The text of this inscription is mentioned by Bees, *op. cit.*, p. 94. For the peculiar division of κοιμη[τήριο]|ν, compare *I.G.*, III, 3453.

34 (Plate X). Inscribed plaque of blue marble, found on February 3, 1936, in Section N. The stone is broken on all sides.

Height, 0.09 m.; width, 0.09 m.; thickness, 0.026 m.

Inv. No. I 3326. ↑

It may well be that the monogram belongs to an architectural block and not to a tombstone; see above, note 87 and p. 16.

XIII. CONCORDANCE OF THE PUBLICATIONS

In order to facilitate further study of the early Christian inscriptions from Athens, a table of concordances, listing the more important collections, has been appended. Whenever possible, the inventory number of the Epigraphical Museum and a reference to later publications have been added.

I.G., III	E. M.	Bayet	Later Publications	*I.G.*, III	E. M.	Bayet	Later Publications
1383	9928/9	118		3453		3	
1384	9940	41		3454	9890/1	25	
1385		98		3455	9888/9	4	
1386	9876	38		3456	9941	24	
1387	9930	80		3457		104	*I.G.*, II², 13240
1427 *b, c*	12003	42	*I.G.*, II², 13216, *B, C*	3458		49	
1428		32		3459	9892	77	
1449	10743	99	*I.G.*, II², 13075	3460		68	
1455	12220	120	*Supra*, note 1	3461	9893	69	
1467		43	*I.G.*, II², 12825	3462	9894	15	
3435	9868	75		3463	9895	17	
3436	9869	21		3464	9897	2	
3437	9870	51	No. I	3465	9898	8	No. III
3438		66	No. II	3466	9896	16	
3439	9771	50		3467	9900/1	5	
3440	9871	65		3468		19	
3441	9872	91		3469			
3442		39		3470	9942	18	
3443		97		3471	9951	59	
3444	9873	44		3472	9899	85	
3445		101		3473	9902		
3446		103		3474	9903	61	
3447		28		3475	9904	20	
3448		36		3476	9907	70	
3449	9874	67		3477	9908	57	
3450		125		3478	9905/6	86	
3451	9875	40		3479		54	
3452		6		3480		46	

I.G., III	E.M.	Bayet	Later Publications	I.G., III	E.M.	Bayet	Harmonia	Later Publications
3481a	9909	71		3529	9939	26		
3481b	2252	55	No. I	3530	9876	94		
3482	9910/1			3531	7877/8 [204]	76		
3483		47		3532	9883	88		
3484	9912	27		3533	5800	124		C.I.I., I, no. 714
3485		14		3534	9879			
3486	9913/4			3535				
3487	9915	83	No. IV	3536	9881/2	45		
3488	9943	22		3537	9884			
3489		31		3538	9698			
3490				3539	9880			
3491	9921	90		3540	9886			
3492	9920	89		3541	9885			
3493		52		3542		33		
3494	9919			3543	5751	63		
3495				3544	9948	92		
3496	9918	73		3545	9927	121		C.I.I., I, no. 712
3497	9917			3546	9887	122		C.I.I., I, no. 713
3498	9916	7		3547	9949/50	123		C.I.I., I, no. 715
3499	9922			3856	9926			
3500	9923	72				10		Supra, note 7
3501		58				11		No. X
3502	9944	37	No. V		4258	13		No. XI
3503		34				56		
3504		62				60		
3505 [202]	9924	29			9967	79	2	No. XII
3506		9			9977	81	19	No. XIII
3507		30				82		
3508		53			3062	84		
3509	9925	107			9982	87	31	No. XIV
3510					9988	95	20	No. XV
3511		64				106		
3512		12	No. VI		9954	108		I.G., VII, 175
3513	9932	102				109		I.G., VII, 170-171
3514	9933	96				110		I.G., VII, 176
3515	3474					111		I.G., VII, 178
3516	9935	74				112		
3516a [203]	9934		No. VII			113		I.G., VII, 177
3517	9936	23	No. VIII			114		
3518	9937	35			9953	115		I.G., VII, 174
3519	9949	119				116		I.G., VII, 172
3520						117		I.G., VII, 173
3521/2	9946	1			9964/5		1	
3523	9947	93			9966		3	No. XVII
3524					9968		4	No. XVIII
3525	9938	78			49		5	No. XIX
3526		48			9969		6	No. XX
3527		105			9971		7	
3528		100			678		8	

[202] Reference to Koumanoudes is no. 3619, and not 3169 as in I.G., III.
[203] Reference to Koumanoudes is 'Αθήναιον, VI, 1877, pp. 384-385, and not p. 7 as in I.G., III.
[204] Squeeze at the Institute for Advanced Study is marked 3877.

I.G., III	E. M.	Harmonia	Later Publications	I.G., III	E. M.	Harmonia	Later Publications
	9970	9	No. XXI		9987	25	
	9972	10	No. XXII		9957	26	*Supra*, pp. 2-3
	9994	11			9989	27	
	9973	12	*Supra*, p. 44			28	
	9963	13	*Supra*, pp. 2-3		9978	29	
	9995	14	*Supra*, note 12		9984	30	
	9976	15	No. XXIII		9983	32	
	9959	16	*Supra*, pp. 2-3		9985	33	*Supra*, note 12
	9960	17	*Supra*, pp. 2-3		9986	34	
	9974	18	*Supra*, note 12		9996	35	*Supra*, note 12
	9979	21		4658 + 9922/3		36	*Supra*, note 12
	9981	22	*Supra*, pp. 49-50		9990	37	*Supra*, note 12
	9980	23			9992	38	*Supra*, note 12
		24					

PRINCETON UNIVERSITY

YALE UNIVERSITY

JOHN S. CREAGHAN, S.J.

A. E. RAUBITSCHEK

EPIGRAPHICAL INDEX OF NAMES

SACRED NAMES

Ἰ(ησοῦ)ς, 49, No. 31
Κύρι(ο)ς, 32, No. XVI
Κ(ύρι)ος, 49, No. 33

[Σω]τήρ, 49, No. 33
Χ[(ριστό)ς], 49, No. 31
Χ(ριστός), 11 [59]

NAMES OF PERSONS

Ἀγαθοκλ[(ῆς or εία)], Corinth, 3[11]
Ἀγαθοκλία, 39, No. 5
Ἀγά[πη], 41, No. 8 b
[Ἀ]θήνεος, 29, No. X
Ἀλαιξ[ά]νδρα, 25, No. I
Ἀλέξω[ν], 26, No. V b
Ἀνδρέας, 29, No. XI, 36, No. XXII, 38, No. 3, 39, No. 5
Ἀγ[δ]ρέας, 21 [131]
[Ἀ]νδ[ρέας], 45, No. 18
[Ἀν]δρέας, 21 [130]
[Ἀνδ]ρέας, 39, No. 4
Ἀνικητία, 30, No. XIII

Γενεθλία, 33, No. XVIII

Διμήτρι[ος], 20 [118]
Διογένης, 37, No. XXIII
Διονύσιος, 27, No. VI
Διονυσόδωρος, 40, No. 6

[Εἰ]ουλλιανός, 14 [71]; cf. p. 20
Ἐλπι[δία (?)], 21 [131]
Ἐλπίδ[ιος (?)], 40, No. 7.
Ἐνέχλια, 32, No. XVII
Ἐπαγάθη, 4 [18]
Ἐπά[γαθος], 50
Ἑρμῆς, 21 [135]
Ἔρουλοι, 35, No. XX
[Εὐ]γένη[ς], 31, No. XIV
Εὐκαρπία, 41, No. 9
Εὐκά[ρπιο]ς, 41, No. 8 b
Εὐτροπία, 40, No. 6
Εὔτυχος, 25, No. I
Εὐφη[μία], 26, No. IV
Εὐφρό[συνο]ς, 41, No. 10

Ζωσιμιανή, 27, No. VII

Ḥ[– – –], 42, No. 12 b

[Θεοδ]ούλη, 41, No. 11
Θεοδώρητος, 37, No. 1
[Θεόφ]αντ[ος], 46, No. 21

[Ἰ]ουλλιανός, 20; cf. 14 [71]
Ἰσίδωρος, 31, No. XV
Ἰωάνης, 21 [133]
[Ἰω]άνης, 41, No. 9
Ἰωά⟨ν⟩νης, 32, No. XVII
Ἰωά[ννης], 36, No. XXI
[Ἰω]ά[ν]νης, 21 [134]

Καλ[3-4]ης, 26, No. V a
Κληby, 26, No. V a
Κλημάτιος, 9
Κυριακός, 28, No. VIII

[Λέων], 41, No. 11

Μ(αρία), 11 [59]
Μαρτυρία, 30, No. XII
Μαρτυρία, 25, No. II
Μαρτύριος, 30, No. XII
Μελιτί[α], 7 [33]
Μελ[ιτία], 36, No. XXI
Μενοι[– – –], 8 [41]

Νίκ(αι)ος, 25, No. III

Ὀνησᾶς, 4 [18]
Ὀνησιφόρος, 38, No. 2
Ọ[– – –], 42, No. 12 b

PLATE I

I

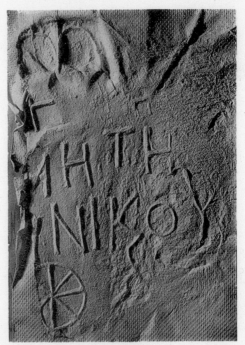

III

V

IV

VI

Nos. I, III-VI (all from Squeezes)

PLATE II

VII

VIII

IX

XII

XIII

Nos. VII-IX, XII-XIII (all from Squeezes)

PLATE III

XI

XVII

XV

XVI

XIV

Nos. XI, XIV–XVII (all from Squeezes)

PLATE IV

XVIII

XIX

XX

XXI

Nos. XVIII-XXI (all from Squeezes)

PLATE V

Nos. XXII-XXIII, 1-4, 6-7 (No. 3 from the Stone, the rest from Squeezes)

PLATE VI

Nos. 5, 8-11 (No. 10 from the Stone, the rest from Squeezes)

PLATE VII

12

13

15 (from Stone)

15 (from Squeeze)

Nos. 12-13 (from Squeeze) and 15

PLATE VIII

14

16

18

EM 9973 (cf. No. 15)

17

20

19

Nos. 14, 16-20, and EM 9973 (Nos. 17-19 from the Stone, the rest from Squeezes)

PLATE IX

Nos. 21-29 (No. 22 from Squeeze, the rest from the Stone)

PLATE X

EM 9981 (cf. No. 33)

Nos. 30-34 and EM 9981 (Nos. 30-31, 33 from the Stone, the rest from Squeezes)